HENRY LELAND

Henry Martyn Leland, 1843-1932

HENRY LELAND:
The Story of the Vermonter
Who Created Cadillac and Lincoln

Gloria May Stoddard

The New England Press
Shelburne, Vermont

Library of Congress Catalog Card Number: 86-61322
ISBN: 0-933050-39-9

The New England Press
P.O. Box 575
Shelburne, Vermont 05482

Cover photograph: Henry Martyn Leland with 1905 Cadillac "Osceola" in 1930 when Leland was 87 years old. Photograph courtesy of Cadillac Motor Car Company.

Printed in the United States of America

Preface

It was in 1962 that I first heard about Henry Martyn Leland from Roy Leonard (now deceased) of Barton, Vermont. I'd been married only a few weeks when we visited my husband's great-uncle Roy and great-aunt Grace (also deceased), who were brother and sister and lived on the family farm. Unknown to me at the time, this visit would turn out to be the beginning of an exciting, 24-year project.

Uncle Roy loved to talk about family history, and before long he began telling me about his grandfather Carlos Leland, who was second cousin to Henry Martyn Leland, the inventor of Cadillac and Lincoln cars. I was amazed by this information as I hadn't known that there was a famous relative in my husband's family.

As Uncle Roy quickly related fact after fact about Henry Leland, I became more and more interested. He'd been born in the same town where I'd been born, married, and now lived. He'd had almost no formal education, yet he'd become the master of precision — the world's foremost automotive engineer.

When I returned home that evening, I immediately started a file on Henry Leland. From that day on I studied every source of information about him that I could find.

During many more visits at the farm, Uncle Roy and Aunt Grace made a wealth of material about Leland available to me. They loaned clippings, newspapers, pamphlets, booklets, and magazines dated from 1886 to 1926. They also loaned me their rare book *Genealogical Record of Henry Leland and His Descendants* which traces the family history up to 1850. These I carefully consulted.

Only facts have been used in this story, but the personal recollections of Aunt Grace and Uncle Roy helped me to develop a feeling of personal acquaintance with Leland. For example, Uncle Roy remembered Henry's extraordinarily large hands and his love for horses. Aunt Grace reminisced about Leland's delight in being served a simple, home-cooked farm meal of garden greens, baking powder biscuits, salt pork gravy, and wild strawberries.

As time went by my fascination with Leland intensified. On Thanksgiving Day 1977 Aunt Grace and Uncle Roy wrote me a letter inviting me to the farm to look at their collection of old pictures of Leland which had been taken during his last visit to Vermont. These had been given to their mother, Leona Leland Leonard, by Henry's son Wilfred in December of 1916.

Through their Victorian old-type parlor stereoscope — consisting of a rack with a wooden handle, a slide for holding each double photograph, and a pair of screened lens-prisms to look through — I studied with great interest 31 view cards of Leland and his family, scenes of Barton, and his son's home in Detroit called "Wilchester."

These three-dimensional pictures were wonderful treasures. Two identical photographs were mounted side by side. Viewed through the stereoscope, the images of people, animals, buildings, and scenes appeared lifelike. A note had been written on the back of each picture giving a brief description.

A year later on October 21, 1978 Aunt Grace and Uncle Roy gave Charlotte free-lance photographer Mary G. Lighthall and me permission to copy for publication their collection of stereopticon views.

The following year I wrote my first article about Leland. It was the feature story in the February 1980 issue of *Good Reading* magazine. This was followed by a full-page article in the *Newport Daily Express*. Both articles were illustrated with copies of stereopticon views from Grace and Roy Leonard's rare collection. Eventually, I wrote a children's story about Leland which is out to market at the time of this writing.

On the third Sunday in January 1978 Aunt Grace and Uncle Roy loaned me a packet of original letters which had been written by Henry Leland to their mother from 1904 through 1930. Here were friendly treasures, indeed. Leland's typewritten letters were full of gratitude, optimism, warmth, and loving-kindness. There were also letters from Leland's son Wilfred, and hand-written ones from his daughter Gertrude. Reading these deepened my understanding and admiration for Leland.

Eventually, Aunt Grace gave me these letters to keep, along with the 1886-1926 resource materials.

As the years passed, I became more and more grateful to folks who save things. I was given a gold-printed invitation announcing a celebration at 156 Lockwood Street, Providence, Rhode Island, on November 5, 1877, honoring Leland's father and mother, Leander and Zilpha Leland, on their 50th Wedding Anniversary. Then in 1977, Mary Greene Lighthall gave me an old, tiny blue book put out by the Cadillac Motor Car Company which she'd found in the attic of her childhood home at Morrisville, Vermont. She also surprised me with a pair of 1892 hair clippers which had been invented by Leland and produced by the Brown & Sharpe Company.

Finally, I received engraved greeting cards which Leland had sent to his Vermont relatives. The verse on one such card, sent to my husband's great-grandmother on Christmas 1922, expresses well the high Christian ideals which Leland upheld in his life and his work. Written by S. D. Gordon, it says in part: "May we crowd out everything that crowds Him out... And lift Him up in sight of everyone we touch."

Helped by Mrs. Adelaide Prangley (now deceased) at the Haskell Free Library at Derby Line, Vermont, who secured research material requested, and by close friends and family members who encouraged me, I gave Henry Martyn Leland my complete attention. Writing this biography of Vermont's "Grand Old Gentleman of Detroit" has been a challenging and rewarding experience which spanned more than two decades.

Over the years, I've become greatly indebted to many people. I wish to express sincere gratitude to: Mr. James J. Bradley, Curator National Automotive History Collection, Detroit Public Library, and Mrs. Vicki Longwish, Cadillac Motor Car Division, General Motors Corporation, both of Detroit, Michigan; Mrs. Cynthia Read-Miller and Mr. Dave Crippen, The Edison Institute, Henry Ford Museum and Greenfield Village, Dearborn, Michigan; Mr. Gary Putnam, National Rifle Association, Washington, D.C.; Mr. John Buechler, Head Special Collections, University of Vermont Bailey-Howe Memorial Library, Burlington, Vermont; and Mrs. Lillian Hoyt, retired Head Librarian of the Jones Memorial Library, Orleans, Vermont.

Grateful acknowledgment is also made to the following: Mr. and Mrs. Maurice Leland, Natick, Massachusetts; Dr. and Mrs. George Leland and Mr. John Houston, all of Orleans, Vermont; Mr. Kenneth Barber, West Glover, Vermont; Mr. Wayne Armstrong, West Charleston, Vermont; Miss Blair Williams, Jericho, Vermont; Miss Ila Carpenter, Newport, Vermont; and Miss Madeline Russell and Mrs. Dale Kinsley, both of Barton, Vermont.

Special thanks go to my former teachers Mrs. Arlene Leslie of Orleans, Vermont, and Mrs. Greta England Scamman of Stratham, New Hampshire, who inspired and held me to high standards; to my faithful and dear friend Mary G. Lighthall of Charlotte, Vermont, for her constant interest and professional help; and to my aunt Vic Chadburn of Jericho, Vermont, and my mother and father, Iris and Gerald Chadburn, of Irasburg, Vermont, whose loving encouragement has been with me through the years.

Finally, my deepest thanks go to my daughter, Mrs. Christine K. Saenz of Enid, Oklahoma, for her unwavering belief in this book long before it was a reality.

To all concerned, I'm most grateful.

Contents

Vermont Farmboy   3
Henry's Chance   9
Toolmaker for Uncle Sam   14
Guns, Fire and Law   20
Hair Clippers   26
Difficult Blows   35
Searching   40
Leland Goes into Business   45
The Cadillac Car   52
A School for Mechanics   59
Rewarding Test   63
Birth of an Electrical System   69
The Secret Engine   79
Homecoming   87
A Loyal American   91
The Lincoln Car   99
"Detroit's Best Citizen"   107
List of Works Consulted   111
About the Author   115

To my children
Christine and Roger Dean
with love

HENRY LELAND

Chapter 1

Vermont Farmboy

On a warm summer day in 1849 six-year-old Henry Leland hurried through the apple orchard to get the herd of cows from the pasture. The sun was low in the afternoon sky, and the only sound in the quiet country air was the distant song of a hermit thrush.

With his heart pounding, Henry raced toward the edge of the woods where the animals were grazing beneath the sugar maples. For an instant, fear froze his legs. Wild bears roamed that dark, dense woods. He'd heard them from his bed late at night. What if one came out of the woods now to attack him and the cows?

Trembling, yet determined to get the cows home safe, he raced and shouted after them, chasing them frantically toward the barn. When they reached the gate, he hastily flung down the stout poles, scattering them noisily right and left. Then he ran to drive the animals into the barnyard.

But all at once his mother appeared by the open gate. "Henry," she called, "come back."

Zilpha Leland, an attractive woman, was a Friend so she had quiet Quaker ways. "Do it like this," she said, stacking the poles neatly to one side of the gate, "so the cows won't get hurt or break the poles."

When she finished, she looked straight into her small son's eyes. "There is a right way and a wrong way to do everything," she told him. "Hunt for the right way, and then go ahead."

His mother's words would direct Henry's thoughts and actions every day of his life. Suddenly his fear was gone. Carefully, he drove the cows through the gate and into the barn. In the years to come he would become the world's foremost automotive engineer — the inventor of Cadillac and Lincoln cars. Letters would reach him from all over the world addressed simply: "Henry Leland, U.S.A."

But after supper that night back in 1849, Henry ran to the small sitting room where his father, Leander Leland, was resting. Mr. Leland was a tall man with a handsome face and full beard. A skilled driver of a team of eight Morgans, he loved horses with a passion. Unfortunately, the strenuous life of the freight route had caused him to suffer from increasingly poor health. This meant he could no longer drive. Regretfully, he had gone back to full-time farming.

Henry Leland, at 73, sitting beside the home of his childhood in Barton, Vermont

Henry Martyn Leland, born in Barton, Vermont, on February 16, 1843, was the youngest child of the Leland household and was named for a famous English missionary to India. Like his father, he too loved horses, and he liked nothing better than to hear stories about the eight-Morgan team.

Listening to Mr. Leland vividly describe his trips between Boston and Montreal, Henry imagined he had been there himself. In his mind, Henry could hear his father commanding the eight horses to pull five-ton wagonloads over the rough dirt roads which wound through the maple woods.

For the hundredth time Mr. Leland told an eager audience of Henry, Edson, Maryanne, and Frank about the hemlock bark, pearlash, and baking soda he carried south, and about the dry goods and West India goods he brought back with him to distribute at places in northern Vermont.

The roads were so bad that the horses could only go five to eight miles each day. In the spring, the wagon wheels often sunk to their hubs in mud. Worse yet, the roads were first bare then snow-covered, so that wheels had to be frequently changed for sled runners. All this, naturally, taxed the strength of all freight drivers and their horses. So every few miles they had to stop to rest at inns along the stagecoach route.

"Times I've seen 150 horses at one barn in one night," Mr. Leland said. "Next morning we'd get up early to feed, clean, card, and harness them. Then we'd be off again."

At such happy story-telling times Henry almost forgot they were living in poverty, with everyone working hard to survive. When Mr. Leland was 21-years-old he'd inherited his father's farm. But an acquaintance had persuaded him to mortgage it and use the money to go into the cattle business with him. Much too generous for his own good, Mr. Leland had trusted the man with his money. One day he discovered that his partner had vanished, leaving him heavily in debt.

Mortgage paying became a terrifying problem. To help pay off the debt, Leland had become a freight driver. The first overnight stop on his route had usually been the stagecoach inn at Glover, now the Union House Nursing Home. It was there he'd met and fallen in love with Zilpha Tifft, the inn-keeper's daughter. They soon married and began raising a family.

With the children's help Mrs. Leland ran the farm. But even with the extra $15 a month Mr. Leland earned as a freight driver, the Lelands hadn't been able to make ends meet. With foreclosure on the mortgage, they were forced to leave the family farm.

Word came from Worcester, Massachusetts, from their married daughter, Sylvia, that work might be available there. With hopes high they'd made the long journey south. But no jobs could be found, and they returned to Barton penniless.

As a last resort, they moved to a farm owned by Mr. Leland's nephew, Joe. This gave them half a small farmhouse for a home and half the profits from the farm. But when the money was divided, it was scarcely enough to live on.

Furthermore, Joe was an alcoholic who beat his wife and frightened his children. Because Leander and Zilpha Leland wished to rear their children to be kind and frugal, living in the same house with Joe was almost unbearable. Desperately, they searched for an escape from their dilemma.

Chapter 2
Henry's Chance

Massachusetts was booming with industry in 1850. It soon turned out that Henry's family found work there. They moved to the large Merrifield estate near Worcester where Mrs. Leland was hired as a nurse. Mr. Leland found work at a nearby grist mill.

Nineteen-year-old Frank got a job in a cobbler shop. Maryanne, 14, and Edson, 11, did odd jobs. Even Henry, who was only eight, earned a small wage feeding and watering 400 chickens and sorting the hundreds of eggs of several fancy breeds of poultry.

Previously, the Leland children had gone to school for only a few months during the summer. Now Edson and Henry could attend school regularly.

One day, however, Frank came home from work carrying a huge wooden box. "Want another job?" he asked his youngest brother.

Of course Henry did.

"The cobbler will pay you three cents for every pair of shoes you peg," Frank said, opening the box full of shoes.

At first the work went slowly, but Henry persisted. Before too long he was fastening soles to shoes with small pieces of wood enthusiastically. When 60 pair of shoes were finished, Henry received his dollar and eighty cents pay. Then Frank brought home another box of shoes.

This business of pegging soles fascinated and challenged Henry. Peg after peg, shoe after shoe, box after box, he began wishing he could work all the time. So one day he discussed the matter with his father and mother. Both insisted he should stay in school. But regretfully they gave their consent because the money was sorely needed.

The months passed quickly. Now 11 and as tall and strong as a man, Henry found a full-time job in Worcester at a factory which made heavy shoes for southern slaves. Seeking for a way to improve the method, he asked himself how he could peg the heavy soles faster while at the same time doing it better. Each day, working beside grown men, he searched for the answer.

In a short time, he found the solution. His time-saving system allowed him to deftly peg the soles of 50 pair of work shoes in a day for which he earned $1.50 — just 25 cents less than the most skilled, grown-up workers!

When Henry was 14, his family moved to the

city of Worcester into a huge white house so Mrs. Leland could take in boarders. The house had a large front porch and spacious lawn. Mr. Leland found employment at Crompton Loom Works where Edson and Henry also began work in the wheel department. Frank ran a planer in a machine shop, and Maryanne married Charles May.

Despite their poverty and Leander Leland's frail health, these were happy times for the devoted and courageous Leland family. They attended church regularly and the kindly pastor, Reverend Jerald, was deeply concerned about all the young people in his church. He was especially interested in young Henry Leland.

One day Reverend Jerald decided to pay Mr. Gordon a visit at Crompton Loom Works. "Henry is no ordinary boy," the pastor advised his friend. "He's been blessed with skillful hands, and his head is full of ideas. He's a hard worker, too. If I were you, I'd make him an apprentice-mechanic."

The superintendent sat back and thought hard a minute. "I guess you're right," he agreed.

However, when Henry was offered the apprenticeship, he did not leap at the chance. Ten hours a day, six days a week — for less pay than he was making now — he'd be shut up indoors with noisy machinery.

Henry was deeply troubled. His work at the wheel department cutting wooden spokes to the same lengths all day long was monotonous. Mr. Gordon's offer was a generous chance for him to learn a trade. But he missed the hours spent out-of-doors. In his own mind he was sure that he would someday be a farmer.

At last Henry agreed to give it a try for two weeks. With a few tools in an old bucket and deep misgivings in his heart, he began his apprenticeship at Crompton Loom Works.

In those days English mechanics were considered superior to American mechanics. England was well ahead of America in the textile industry. At Crompton Loom Works most of Henry's shopmates were older, skilled Englishmen. So when the inexperienced Henry made a mistake, as all apprentices must, his seasoned shopmates laughed at him loudly. "What can you expect of a Yankee?" his foreman jeered, throwing up his hands in a gesture of helplessness. "Thou'lt never be a mechanic, lad."

Young Henry flushed with resentment, but he never wavered from his determination to do his best. He persisted long after the two-week trial period was over. Day after day he worked quickly and quietly over the giant looms, determined to become a good mechanic. He learned something new about the machines all the time and began to enjoy the precise, creative work.

Despite the daily rejection of his superiors he advanced quickly. He began stopping at the library after work. One night as he chose an adventure novel, a stranger exclaimed, "Surely you don't read that trash!"

"What better use can I make of my time than to

read?" Henry hotly retorted.

"It makes a lot of difference *what* you read," the stranger told him frankly. He led Henry to another section of the library and helped him select a couple of excellent volumes.

With the exception of the Bible, Henry had never read any outstanding books. Now, at the stranger's suggestion, he began reading about Eli Whitney, Robert Fulton, and Thomas Jefferson.

Ideas began to buzz in Henry's head. Soon he astonished Mr. Gordon and his expert shopmates by becoming the most talented apprentice-mechanic at Crompton Loom Works!

One evening when Henry was 16, he attended an illustrated lecture at his church. Afterward, Reverend Jerald introduced him to Elias Hull, a farmer, and his pretty, brown-haired daughter, Ellen.

As soon as the friendly young "Nelle" met the tall, handsome mechanic, she began to fall in love with him. Soon he fell in love, too, and loved her devotedly the rest of his life.

Chapter 3
Toolmaker For Uncle Sam

The struggle between the North and South over slavery had become so bitter that there seemed little hope of settling the issue without war. Grieved though he was, 20-year-old Edson Leland did not hesitate. He volunteered for the Union Army.

Fiercely patriotic, Henry wanted to join, too. But because he was under age, he had to ask his parents for their permission.

"No," Mr. Leland objected.

"You are only 17," Mrs. Leland quietly pointed out.

Typically, Henry was obstinate. Alone with Edson, he exploded, "It's not fair! You're getting a chance to serve our country, and I'm as strong as you! Please come with me to the recruiting office? I *must* enlist!"

Although Edson understood Henry's intense

loyalty to the Union and his passionate devotion to President Abraham Lincoln, he shook his head helplessly. "Mother says you're too young to go to war."

"But Mother is wrong!" Henry persisted stubbornly. "I'll *be* old enough my next birthday!"

Edson gazed fondly at his confident young brother and was suddenly struck by the truth of his words. No recruiting officer would question Henry's age. He was more than six feet tall and broad-shouldered, with powerful arms and huge hands. And Edson had never known anyone who possessed such unlimited energy. In fact, Henry seemed completely tireless in spite of the long, hard hours he worked.

There was no doubt about it. Henry would make a good soldier — probably even better than himself. Edson decided Henry was right. He agreed to help him.

Secretly, the brothers made their way to the recruiting office. But when they arrived, they discovered that their mother had guessed their plan. She had come earlier to record Henry's proper age.

On February 16, 1861, Henry turned 18. By Thursday, April 11, industry had sagged so badly that nearly all the men at Crompton Loom Works were dismissed, but Henry's employers were legally obliged to keep their apprentices. The next day, Confederate troops attacked Fort Sumter. President Lincoln, who was Henry's hero, issued a call for 75,000 additional soldiers.

Again Henry wanted to join. But by now he had become so valuable to the government as a toolmaker that he was exempt from military duty.

Unexpectedly, it turned out that Mr. Crompton and Mr. Gordon had accepted an important government contract to make Blanchard lathes that were used to make gun stocks at Federal armories. Henry was Crompton's most skilled apprentice, and Mr. Gordon trusted him completely. In order to manufacture Blanchard lathes, delicate machine tools had to be produced. These tools required the highest degree of accuracy known in the toolmaking industry.

This precision job was given to Henry Leland.

Humbly accepting the special task, Henry's thoughts went back to when he was six-years-old and his fear of bears had caused him to be careless with the gate poles. "There is a right way and a wrong way to do everything," his mother had told him then. "Hunt for the right way, and then go ahead. In that way the cows won't get hurt." Now Henry applied her practical advice.

Another apprentice, Jill Backson, watched Henry as he diligently worked on the vital machine tools. "You're too careful, Leland," he said testily.

"It has to be done right," Henry returned.

Jill continued to fume. "You're turning out too much work. Why don't you slow down? The rest of us can't keep up with you. No one is paying you any extra to break your back, so why work so hard?"

Young Backson was constantly stirring up

trouble in the shop. While it was true Henry was faster and more accurate than the other apprentices and he was receiving no extra money in spite of the government assignment, the pay didn't really matter to him. The important thing was *quality*. The Springfield rifle was the principal rifle of the Northern Army. It was carried by his brother Edson, and Confederate soldiers as well. No soldier was going to get hurt because of carelessness on Henry's part.

When the rare tools were finished, the officers from the United States Armory at Springfield came to inspect them. Henry could feel his heart pounding with excitement.

Then his eyes shone with pride and joy when he saw the looks of approval on the inspectors' faces. "Good work, Leland!" said the superior officer, smiling and shaking the young mechanic's hand.

"Thank you, sir. Thank you," Henry kept repeating.

The officer waved his thanks aside. "We're short of expert mechanics. Anytime you decide to come to Springfield, we'd be privileged to give you a job at the Armory."

This proud moment was rudely shattered when Mr. and Mrs. Leland received notice that Edson had come down with swamp fever on the Chickahominy River in Virginia. He was captured by the Confederates, sent to Libby Prison in Richmond, then finally released to the New York City Hospital. But he died there in September.

Edson's death at the age of 22 was a terrible

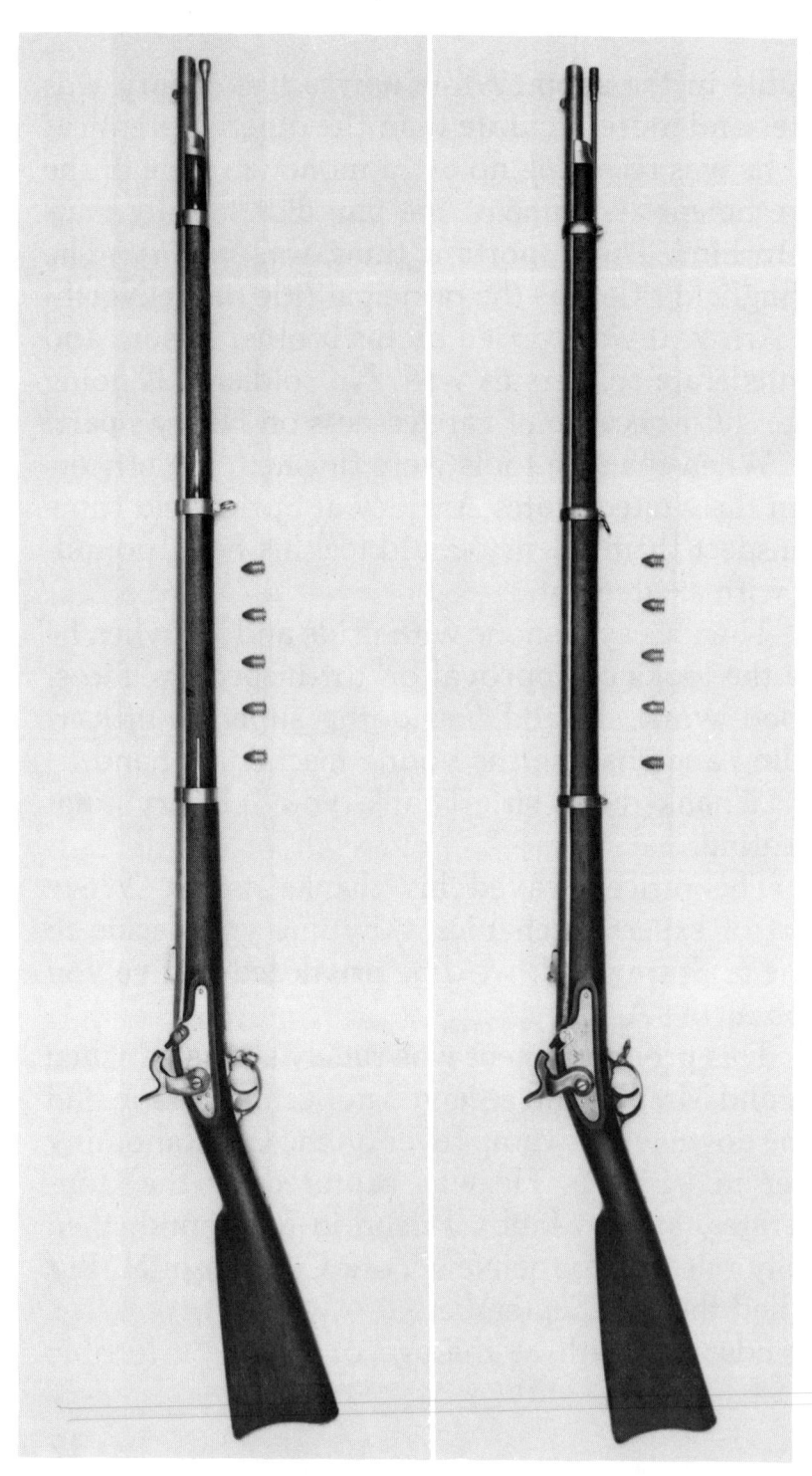

Top: Model 1861 Springfield rifle like the ones Leland built at the Springfield Armory. Bottom: Model 1863 Springfield rifle like the ones Leland built at the Springfield Armory.

shock to the close-knit Leland family. Numb with grief, Henry left Worcester for Springfield.

In those days most factories and machine shops were dirty and cluttered. The United States Armory at Springfield, however, was clean and orderly. There, accepting even lower wages than he had received at Crompton Loom Works, Henry was taught the valuable Eli Whitney system of interchangeable parts and machine tooling. In the years to come, he looked back on the training with a profound sense of gratitude.

All during the Civil War years Henry drove himself furiously making parts for the .58 caliber, muzzle-loading, one-shot Model 1861 and Model 1863 Springfield rifles. And he wrote long, affectionate letters to Nelle who was attending college to become a teacher.

He was true to his goal. He'd become one of the youngest master mechanics in all New England. He'd done well. Nelle and his working-together family were proud of him.

On February 16, 1864, Henry Martyn Leland celebrated his twenty-first birthday. That November, he voted in a Presidential election for the first time. In Springfield he cast his vote for the man whom he believed to be the greatest of all Americans.

The day he voted for Abraham Lincoln was a proud day for him. He was never to forget it. Nor would he ever forget the next April of 1865 when President Lincoln was assassinated.

Chapter 4
Guns, Fire and Law

With Lee's surrender at Appomattox, Henry Leland's work at the United States Armory at Springfield ended. When the Armory closed, he traveled by train along the Connecticut River to Hartford where he immediately began work at the Colt Revolver Factory.

The clean, well-lighted armory at Hartford had been built by Colonel Samuel Colt just a few years before his death in 1862. It was the biggest private armory in the world, manufacturing pocket and holster pistols, hunting rifles and shotguns, and special police and military models.

Leland soon discovered that Colt's interchangeable manufacturing was advanced even further than at the Federal Armory at Springfield. And on several occasions he was told, "Every part of a Colt must be perfect," for here Samuel Colt's famous tradition must be followed precisely each day.

Although Leland thrived on precision and gained valuable experience every day, his future continued to trouble him. By now he and Nelle were engaged, yet they were miles away from each other. He was finding the separation harder and harder to bear.

Once again, he gave serious thought to farming. Luckily, he had been able to save some money. But was it enough to buy a farm and support a wife and family?

The lonely months dragged on. Then one day Henry received great news from Nelle. "At last I have completed my college teaching course," she wrote from her father's farm. This news delighted Henry. Impulsively, he left Hartford and returned to Worcester so he could be near Nelle.

It was good to be back home, and he soon found a job working for Augustus Prouty, a manufacturer of card-setting machinery used for weaving. Nelle began teaching school, and at last the engaged couple set their wedding date for late September, 1867.

A few weeks later, Mr. Prouty decided to promote his card-setting machine at the World's Fair. Because he trusted Leland completely, he put him in charge of the office. "There is money in the bank, and more will soon come in from machinery sales," Mr. Prouty told his newly appointed office manager. Then he went off to Europe.

Unfortunately, the sales Mr. Prouty had expected were not forthcoming. Soon the money in the bank was gone, leaving none for the payroll. Henry was friends with all the workmen, and he knew that they needed their wages immediately in order to feed their families; but there was no way to reach Prouty and no one else to turn to.

Worried and torn by doubts, he could see only one way out of the emergency. Believing that Mr. Prouty would repay him when he returned from Europe, Leland took money from his own savings and paid the men their wages.

But to Leland's bitter disappointment, when Mr. Prouty returned from the World's Fair he was broke. His business soon went bankrupt, and Henry not only lost his hard-earned savings but his job as well.

He was stunned. It had been eight years since he and Nelle had met and fallen in love, Now, with his savings gone, a farm seemed completely out of the question. Nevertheless, they decided to wait no longer to be married. Undaunted, their wedding took place as planned on September 25th.

During the next five years, Leland made short stabs at three more jobs in Worcester. First he worked at the Loring Coes Wrench Works, then the Lucius W. Pond Tool Company, and finally the Charles H. Ballard Rifle Company.

In addition, he joined the Worcester City Fire Department. Dressed in his fireman's uniform — a flaming red shirt, dark trousers with red stripes down the sides, and a shiny, patent leather belt with huge brass buckle — Nelle thought Henry was the handsomest man she'd ever seen.

In those days fighting fire was even more strenuous than it is today. Sometimes horses could not be quickly found to pull the cumbersome fire engines. Then the firemen, 40 strong, had to pull them. Water had to be pumped by hand, and often relayed from man to man. Worse yet was the fierce competition between fire companies.

Henry was the tongue man or spokesman for the Rapid Company No. 2. Its worst rival, the Tiger Company No. 6, was constantly stirring up trouble. The result was bitter quarreling and even fist fighting.

Despite their hand-to-mouth existence, these were happy times for the Lelands. They attended church regularly, and Henry became involved in city politics. Frank Leland and his wife gave birth to William Henry Leland, middle-named after his uncle. Then Henry and Nelle became the proud parents of a daughter, Gertrude, followed soon afterward by a son, Wilfred.

Unhappily, these joyous events were succeeded by a crisis. Frustrated by the constant fighting between the Rapid No. 2 and the Tiger No. 6 and nervous from working indoors day after day in noisy machine shops, Henry teetered on the edge of a breakdown. At Nelle's insistence, he took a real vacation for the first time in his life.

Following a peaceful rest at the Hull farm in

Worcester, Henry was refreshed and eager to return to work. But he had made up his mind he would fight with the quarrelsome firemen no more. Nor did he intend to go back to noisy machine shops. But where was he going to find a job?

He was well equipped physically for police work, and he'd had plenty of experience with firearms. In addition, he had taught himself to write and speak well. A friend, who had recently become a judge, convinced him to apply for night duty on the Worcester City Police Force and to study law during the day.

Leland was quickly accepted and issued uniforms and equipment. Gradually, he got into the habit of policing at night and soaking up knowledge of the law during the day. He was having an exciting and busy time. Law fascinated him. In addition to his formal reading, he continued his intensive outside reading about religion and science. It got so that he found less and less time to rest.

One night while he was pacing his beat, he stumbled over a large stone. Startled, he awakened abruptly, alarmed that he had dozed off while on duty.

Early the next morning he paid his doctor a visit. After a thorough examination he was told, "There's nothing wrong with you that sleep won't cure. You're just trying to do too much."

Up to now Leland had never really known what it meant to be tired. Now he found out. Working all night and studying all day, he found little time for either sleep or his family.

At last he was forced to take a long, hard look at his future. He was 29-years-old. His children, aged four and three, were growing fast. His father-in-law, Elias Hull, was an old man now and had retired. Henry and Nelle both loved the Hull farm and desperately longed to buy it. But they were barely able to make ends meet, and there was no money saved.

In truth, Henry Leland was convinced that he should be a farmer. Refusing to be discouraged he told himself stubbornly, "There has to be a way to buy that farm!"

Chapter 5
Hair Clippers

Henry Leland admired Joseph Brown who was known the world over as New England's most outstanding precisionist. So bright and early on the first day of July, 1872, Leland showed up in his one suit — a policeman's uniform — at the Brown & Sharpe Company in Providence, Rhode Island.

Somewhat reluctantly, Leland had made the decision to return to factory work and move his family to Providence. But now, as Mr. Brown showed him around the huge, spotless well-lighted toolmaking factory, Henry felt like he was being shown a bit of heaven.

Here precision standards, accurate to 1/1000th of an inch — or one-third the thickness of one piece of human hair — surpassed even that of Colt's. It was no wonder, Leland thought, that Brown & Sharpe's excellent tools and instruments repeatedly won Grand Prix awards around the world.

At first Leland was put to work making gears and cutters. Because he replaced a man whose relatives were supervisors for the company, he was greatly resented. Almost at once trouble began.

The toolroom attendant, encouraged by most of the other workmen, decided to make things tough for the company's newest mechanic. Every time Leland needed a special tool, which happened fairly often, the attendant gave him a silly argument. The result was that Henry was kept needlessly waiting. This went on day after day until Leland's patience grew thin.

One day he went to the toolroom to get a special part. "Please hand me the center rest," Henry asked politely.

The attendant snorted. "There's no such tool."

"It's right up there," Henry replied, pointing a huge forefinger at the part which hung on the wall behind the impudent man.

After a long moment of silence Leland was rudely informed, "That's a back rest." But no attempt was made to get the tool which Henry needed in order to do his work.

Leland was furious. Making one huge leap over the counter, he grabbed the startled attendant by the collar and gave him a powerful shake. "You have been deliberately making trouble, and this will be the last time that I endure any more nonsense from you," he warned. "The next time you open your mouth for anything but a courteous response,

I'll take you by the neck and throw you through the window — whether it is open or closed!"

There was no more trouble.

Mr. Brown and his partner, Lucien Sharpe, quickly recognized Leland's ability for leadership. As soon as he had become thoroughly familiar with the work of every department, they made him supervisor of the small but important screw machine department.

Although there were only six machines in the unit, here was a chance for Leland to use his unusual skill and independent thinking. But at that time many of his ideas were so revolutionary — like his suggestion to carry screws and small parts in stock — that it took a great deal of time and persuasion to convince Mr. Brown and Mr. Sharpe to put them into operation. Nevertheless, as time went on most of his ideas were accepted. In a few months, he was supervising 60 machines.

One day Brown & Sharpe received an order for several pair of horse clippers. When it was turned over to the screw machine department, Leland gasped in horror. His thoughts shot back to the long, freezing winters in Vermont. How inhuman to clip the hair off horses. They would shiver with cold.

His long legs swiftly carried him to the superintendent's office. "I refuse to have my men make these horse clippers," he blurted out.

The superintendent stared at him in surprise. Henry Leland generally went out of his way to please others. What had struck him?

"It's cruel to clip the hair off a horse in cold weather!" Leland stormed. "I won't fill this order."

"But you must," the superintendent insisted.

"I won't," Leland returned, unyielding.

A long, heated debate followed. At last Leland was convinced that if Brown & Sharpe didn't make the horse clippers, another company would. Finally he relented. "If they *must* be made," he told the superintendent, "I shall see that they are at least made *right* so the horses' hair won't be pulled."

Leland's men made the clippers. Then Henry put them to a test. Since calves had the finest hair of any animal he knew, he got several calfskins and mounted them on boards. He made one complete stroke into the hair with one pair of clippers. Then he drew them out and blew away the loose hairs. If even one single hair caught between the blades, he returned the clippers to one of his men and insisted they be resharpened.

Indeed, as he tested and experimented with every single pair of horse clippers he began to think of new ways to improve the grinding machine. At his first chance he discussed his ideas with the supervisor of the sewing machine department, Richmond Viall.

Mr. Viall then attempted to discuss Leland's ideas, along with his own, with Joseph Brown. But the old inventor was too busy with other important work to pay him close attention.

When every pair of horse clippers had passed

Leland's gruelling calfskin test, he was satisfied. He felt he had done his very best. Then he hurried to Mr. Brown's office to talk about his ideas for an entirely new and special grinding machine. Mr. Brown listened to him and carefully thought about his suggestions. He agreed to meet with him and Richmond Viall later to discuss their ideas more thoroughly.

It soon turned out that Brown & Sharpe's horse clippers were so superior that one day a barber brought a pair to Henry Leland. "Can you make me some clippers like these to cut hair with?" he asked hopefully.

Leland flashed the man a pleasant smile. This was an order he would be *glad* to try to fill. A man could have his hair clipped as short as he pleased and still keep warm by wearing a hat and scarf! But, in truth, he was still deeply worried about horses being clipped and catching cold.

He believed he had done his best with the horse clippers. But now his best appeared to be just good enough. He determined to try to make a better pair of clippers.

Sure enough, he found a way to improve the horse clippers. He added a spring to the center and made them lighter.

"Fine! That's fine!" the barber exclaimed happily, as he squeezed the handles together several times. Grinning, he shook Leland's hand. "Thank you, sir. Thank you." Then he went off to his barber shop completely satisfied.

But Henry wasn't satisfied. The hair clippers

were still far too clumsy to suit him. He decided to delve into it more deeply. Cautiously, he cut and trimmed and sharpened until he was sure that the hair clippers were as lightweight and efficient as he could possibly make them. He decided to have a heart-to-heart talk with Mr. Brown and Mr. Sharpe.

"I believe there's a good market for these," he said enthusiastically, showing his invention to the two men. "If we manufacture these hair clippers, we stand to make a big profit."

Mr. Brown's natural curiosity was aroused. He examined the clippers halfheartedly, but quickly handed them back. "No one would buy those," he murmured. "We'd be wasting our time and money." Mr. Sharpe, the company's business expert, flatly refused to even consider Leland's invention.

Disappointed, the months dragged by. But Leland could not shake off his notion that the hair clippers would be useful to people. He decided to apply for a patent. Consequently, he was the first inventor to receive a patent for barber's clippers.

It was clear, he told himself, that he would have to *find* a market for the hair clippers. The biggest hardware firm he knew about was Dame, Stoddard and Kendall. At his first chance he went to Boston to talk with its owners.

"Wonderful! These are wonderful." Mr. Dame exclaimed excitedly when Leland showed him a pair of his hair clippers. Mr. Dame's partners heartily agreed. "Tell Mr. Brown and Mr. Sharpe to manufacture them. We'll be happy to place a big order right away."

"On second thought," Mr. Dame added, "I'll write and tell them so myself!"

Mr. Dame's enthusiastic letter, recommending that Henry Leland's hair clippers be marketed at once, opened Mr. Brown's and Mr. Sharpe's eyes at last. Two years had passed since Henry first suggested they manufacture his invention. Now they decided it might be worthwhile after all.

The hair clippers Henry Leland invented were an instant success in America. Brown & Sharpe had to create a special department in order to keep up with its production. In no time, they were manufacturing 300 pair of hair clippers a day and orders began pouring in from all over the world. Soon, Leland's invention became one of Brown & Sharpe's most profitable products.

Meanwhile, Leland's bosses thanked him and added a mere 50 cents a day to his pay envelope — though his invention was earning them $1000 a day!

Consequently, the thought of buying a business of his own was even more tempting than ever. But the Hull farm had recently been sold. Besides, Leland still hadn't been able to save any money.

The winter of 1875-1876 was a very hard one. The Lelands sent every extra penny they could spare to Henry's sickly mother and father.

Then, the following July Joseph Brown died suddenly. His Universal Grinder was announced by the Brown & Sharpe Company only a few days

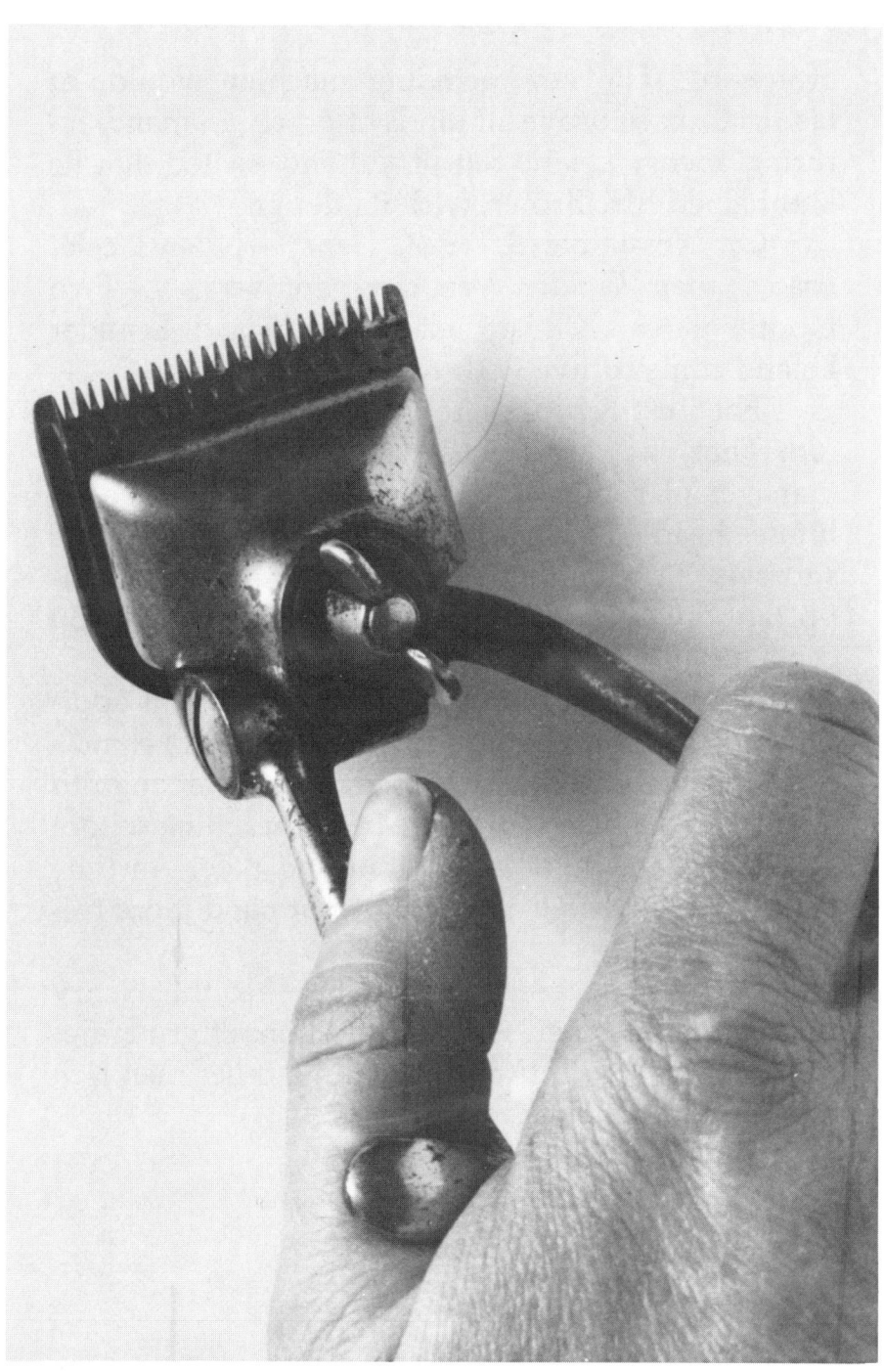

The first barber's clippers, invented by Henry Leland and produced by Brown & Sharpe Company, Providence, Rhode Island.

afterward. The new grinding machine would, at last, greatly improve all kinds of precision manufacturing. Henry Leland felt proud and excited that he had helped Mr. Brown with its design.

On November 5, 1877, Henry's parents celebrated their Golden Wedding anniversary. Two months later, Zilpha Leland died, and Leander Leland came to live with his son and family.

The next February 16, Henry turned 35-years-old. That day, Mr. Viall was promoted to general manager of Brown & Sharpe, and Henry replaced him as head of the sewing machine department. As supervisor of the company's largest and most important division, his pay was again raised a mere 50 cents a day.

Now with an ailing father to support in addition to his wife and two growing children, Leland's small salary of $100 a month was barely enough to get by on. To help out, Nelle began teaching school again. But she soon grew tired and pale. As time went by, she visited the doctor more and more frequently.

Deeply concerned about her health, Henry hired a housekeeper. And he told himself grudgingly, "Perhaps I ought to quit making other men rich and go into business for myself."

Chapter 6
Difficult Blows

The former Hull farm was for sale again. At last in 1880, Henry and Nelle were able to afford the small down payment. It was certain, they told themselves, that the land would produce enough cash crops to make the annual payments. Happily, they moved to the country.

They worked out a plan. Henry would stay in Providence and continue to work at Brown & Sharpe during the week, then travel to Worcester to be with his family each weekend. Meanwhile, Nelle would run the farm with the help of Henry's aging father and Gertrude and Wilfred.

The future looked bright indeed. Ten-year-old Wilfred led the work horse while his grandfather guided the plow. Then they planted a garden and crops. Gertrude, who was 12, fed and watered the animals, tended the chickens, and gathered the eggs.

And, Nelle cooked and cleaned and milked the cows. After a hard week at the noisy factory, Henry arrived at the farm to chop wood, pick stones, and build fences.

When the hay was ready to be cut, the men worked long hours in the field while Nelle weeded the garden and Gertrude picked berries. Later, the whole family toiled in the apple orchard behind the farmhouse, hand-picking and carefully packing thousands of Baldwins and Breenings to be sold at a dollar a barrel.

This happy country living lasted only a few months, however. In the days to come, managing the farm proved too difficult for Nelle and her health failed a second time. Furthermore, Henry desperately longed to be with his family during the week, and the lengthy trips between Providence and Worcester became more and more exhausting.

Gradually, but so painfully, Henry and Nelle faced the fact that their farm crops had earned them very little money.

The date of the annual installment came. But Henry and Nelle had no cash with which to make the payment. There was nothing else to do. They must give up the farm and animals they loved so dearly.

His dream of farming hopelessly shattered, Henry took one last walk through the sweet-smelling woods. The sun was low in the afternoon sky and the pine needles were soft underfoot. The only sound was the song of a distant bird.

With a rebellious mind, Henry sat down on a tree stump in the middle of the quiet woods and took a deep look into his soul. After a long time, he bowed his head and submitted himself to God's will.

Finally, a voice in his innermost mind said, "You were never intended for a farm. The factory is your destined place of work."

Slowly, Henry stood up and began walking back out of the woods, his rebellion gone.

Leland moved his family back to Providence and returned to work wholeheartedly. Machines were his future now. He would master them and make useful things for people. In fact, he resolved to teach his apprentices to do the same.

"Would you like to be a good mechanic, get promoted, and have a better job?" Leland asked each new man he hired. "Then watch closely, and do just as I show you." He made several simple machine pieces exactly right. "Now you make some," he told the young man. "Stay at it until you've made several that are perfect. Then bring them to me." Then he walked quickly away to avoid embarrassment.

When a man had made a number of metal pieces, Leland tested them with a gauge. If they were inferior in any way, he gently told the apprentice to try again. But if the pieces were absolutely perfect he declared: "Now there is no reason why you cannot make a thousand pieces exactly right!"

In those days, Leland's theories on management were revolutionary, but he proved that his method actually cut manufacturing costs in half and greatly increased production. In 1881, he wrote an important paper entitled "The Art of Manufacturing." In the years to follow, it had an enormous impact upon the industrial world.

That same year, Leander Leland died at the age of 79. The following year, Nelle gave birth to a third child. She and Henry named their second daughter Miriam.

A busy year passed. Then one night Henry came home from work tired and hot. His head ached terribly. So did his arms, legs, and back. Lacking his usual good appetite, he went to bed early without eating.

In the morning his face was flushed, and he was running a high temperature. Nelle sent Wilfred for Dr. Stone, and when he arrived, he confirmed Nelle's worst fear — her husband had *typhoid fever!*

In those days typhoid fever was one of the deadliest of diseases. Doctors didn't know about vaccinations and innoculations. All they could do was suggest that their patients be given large amounts of liquids and cold sponge baths to help control the fever.

Three horrible weeks went by. Nelle sat by Henry's bed, sponging him with cool water and praying for him to live. Despite this, he lost weight and his fever steadily rose until it reached 105. Half the time he was delirious and kept mumbling strange things.

Dr. Stone came twice a day, but there was little

he could do. "The fever has to run its course," he explained helplessly.

Then one morning Nelle touched Henry's forehead. It was cool! The worst was over! She burst into tears of joy and gratitude.

It took Henry a long time to recover fully from the attack of typhoid fever.

Chapter 7
Searching

At Dr. Stone's advice, Leland took his family to Columbus, Ohio. They moved into the Neal House, not far from the State Capitol. Henry found light work at the Jordan & Meeham Roller Caster plant and slowly regained his health.

During the months that followed, Leland became convinced that he could help people in government. A whole new world opened up for him at Neal House, a world which was alive with the sound of men's voices as they debated about economics and government.

He became acquainted with Ohio politicians and began attending political meetings. He especially liked and trusted the Republican Congressman William McKinley who shared with Henry a love of horses.

However, his days in Ohio came to an end

when fire destroyed the Jordan & Meeham plant. His job gone, there was nothing for him to do but return to the Brown & Sharpe Company in Providence.

Lucien Sharpe and Richmond Viall lost no time creating a new position for the man who had contributed so much to the company. They made Henry Leland the first shopman to sell machines and tools as a traveling representative to the Midwest.

How Leland's world changed during the next six years, from 1883-1889, as he traveled from Pittsburgh west to Milwaukee, Chicago, and St. Louis, as well as to all the important cities in Ohio, Michigan and Indiana. In his own mind, he never considered himself a salesman. At each factory he simply talked to the businessmen and mechanics about jobs and machines. Never timid about instructing men on the proper use of machinery and tools, he had a way of inspiring his listeners. On several occasions his advice led to a whole new system of manufacturing.

On one of these trips he arrived at the Westinghouse Air Brake Company in Pittsburgh, Pennsylvania, just as an important test was being made in the yard. A man started a locomotive which pulled a long row of passenger cars a short distance down a track. Then he applied the air brakes. Instead of immediately stopping, the train traveled a considerable distance down the track before coming to a final halt.

Unhappily, a crew of mechanics removed the

leaky air brakes from each car, scraped the pistons, then put them back for another trial.

George Westinghouse had only recently invented and perfected the air brake for railroad trains, and Leland watched test after test in fascination. For a long time, he was stumped. Then he found the answer to the problem, and approaching the mechanics he advised, "For such precision work those cylinders and pistons should be ground." Briefly, he explained the process of grinding.

Afterward, Leland hurried to the office of the superintendent to discuss his ideas with Mr. Welch. At first, the deaf superintendent was skeptical of the grinding method. But after a loud, lengthy discussion, Leland somehow convinced him of its merits and was given a number of rough castings to take back to Providence.

Only a few men in the world knew how to produce machine parts to 1/1000th of an inch, and Leland was one of those men. Using the grinding system at Brown & Sharpe, he carefully made a complete set of cylinders and pistons exactly right. Then he hurried back to Pittsburgh.

Westinghouse mechanics replaced their scraped parts from the air brakes of the long train with Leland's perfect parts. Then they watched breathlessly as the locomotive pulled the cars down the track. When the air brakes were applied this time, the air held, and the train pulled to a screeching halt.

Mr. Welch was amazed. He gave Leland an

order for several grinding machines. When Henry suggested a demonstration of the grinding procedure be given by Brown & Sharpe's experienced mechanics, the superintendent flatly refused his generous offer. Consequently, three months after the Brown & Sharpe grinding machines were delivered to the Westinghouse Air Brake Company, Mr. Welch declared them worthless.

When Leland discovered this, he traveled to Pittsburgh at once to demonstrate personally the grinding operation. In a few days, every Brown & Sharpe grinding machine was successfully operating once more, and the air brake became a reliable safety device.

For some time, Joseph Brown's Universal Grinder was both useful and popular, but Leland was not completely satisfied with it. For one thing, it was too light. Secondly, it lacked power and speed. He decided to talk the matter over with a friend at Brown & Sharpe, Charles H. Norton.

The result was that Mr. Norton redesigned the Universal Grinder and made it heavier, stronger, and speedier. When the new grinding machine — called the No. 1 Surface Grinder — appeared on the market in 1886, Henry Leland was proud and excited to have had a part in its creation.

As Leland traveled throughout the Midwest, he became intimate friends with many successful businessmen. From them he learned that a man could establish his own business — without a lot of money — by sharing ownership with a wealthy man who did have funds to invest.

With renewed hope of his old dream to have his own business, he began looking for financial backing and an ideal place to locate a machine shop. He especially favored Chicago and Detroit because they were expanding more rapidly than most major cities in the Midwest.

Leland's work drew him more and more away from his family and made him long to be with those he loved. A deep bond of mutual trust and respect sprung up between Henry and his son who had become a young man by now. From Chicago Henry wrote a letter to Wilfred: "I have had thee in mind these days of our separation and have often wondered what you and sister and Mama were doing at that particular time... I shall be in Milwaukee next Sunday, I expect, and shall from there feel that every move brings me nearer home."

For some time Wilfred had spent his summers and school vacations working at Brown and Sharpe and running errands and collecting bills for Dr. Stone. He always added his wages to the family income. As his mother's health grew steadily worse, he took over the responsibility of the family accounts. In 1889, he entered Brown University and began taking a preparatory course in medicine.

Chapter 8
Leland Goes Into Business

Good fortune struck in the bustling city of Detroit. There Leland became friends with a wealthy toolmaker named Charles Strelinger, who in turn introduced him to Robert Faulconer of Alpena, Michigan.

Somehow Leland convinced the well-to-do Faulconer to invest $40,000 in a machine and toolmaking shop. He borrowed an additional $2,000 from Lucien Sharpe, added his own $1,600 savings, and talked his friend Charles Norton into moving to Michigan.

In Detroit, Henry Leland settled down permanently. He moved his family into a house on North Grand Boulevard and set up the company of Leland, Faulconer, and Norton at the corner of Bates and Congress Streets on the fourth floor of the Strelinger Building. The new machine shop opened for business on September 19, 1890, with 12 employees.

Right away, Leland announced its opening by sending thousands of letters to prospective customers in Michigan, Ohio, and Indiana. Then he wrote a letter to his son in Providence begging him to temporarily leave Brown University and come to Detroit to help get the company started.

Leland's machine shop was an instant success. A steady supply of special tools and machines were ordered, produced, and sold. And, to Henry's delight, Wilfred arrived in Detroit on November 7, 1890 — on his 21st birthday — with the promise to assist his father during his first, difficult year.

Early in 1891, Leland had to hire 48 more men. On several occasions, inventors dropped by to ask advice about working out difficult manufacturing problems. Consequently, the company of Leland, Faulconer, and Norton made the first typewriters, pencil sharpeners, and automatic chicken feeders.

No matter how busy Henry Leland became, he was always honest and fair and genuinely concerned about each one of "his boys" as he called the 60 workmen. They in turn felt a special kinship with him and affectionately referred to their tall, white-haired boss as "Uncle Henry."

Leland held daily conferences to discuss problems and ideas with his foremen. And, because he believed that men must live in close contact with God to be happy human beings, he also led his boys in prayer and Scripture reading sessions every noon.

As in all aspects of his life, Henry's deep Christian beliefs guided his thinking about government. When he discovered that some Detroit politicians engaged in dishonest voting, he was too honest to be silent. A way must be found, he told himself indignantly, to clean up the bad citizenship of good citizens. First he discussed the matter with his secretary, John Bourne. Then he talked to Judge Pliny Marsh. Finally, Henry talked to his boys at Leland, Faulconer, and Norton and to friends and fellow workers at his church. In the end, he successfully organized a group to fight corruption which resulted in getting rid of dishonest politicians, reorganizing city government, and holding honest elections.

By the close of 1891, 22-year-old Wilfred Leland had become his father's devoted and trusted associate. He made the difficult decision to return to Providence — not to continue studying medicine, but to receive additional training as a precision machinist at Brown & Sharpe.

With the help of his father's friend, Richmond Viall, Wilfred did three year's work in just one year. And soon he, too, could machine to 1/1000th of an inch.

No father and son were ever closer than the gifted, strong-willed Henry and the brilliant, sensitive Wilfred Leland. Their combined talents formed a powerful and harmonious team. By 1893 the company had grown so large that they designed and built a new machine shop on Detroit's east side on Twombly Avenue.

By 1894 Henry was able to pay his debts, and he bought out Charlie Norton and some of the other small stockholders. The company was reorganized as Leland & Faulconer and became known locally as "L & F."

Then sorrow struck. Miriam Leland's life ended at the age of 12. The whole family grieved but they were consoled by their strong belief in eternal life.

Somehow Henry thrust aside his agony and tried to solve an urgent business problem. From the first, no midwestern foundry could produce iron castings to suit him. Valuable time was wasted ordering them from Brown & Sharpe, the only eastern company which could.

Henry was positive that his company needed a foundry of its own. Before long, he convinced the other stockholders to build a foundry onto the machine shop. When it was completed, in 1896, it was the first in the West to equal Brown & Sharpe's precision-machined castings.

Leland had complete faith in himself and the men he trained. But it was part of his belief that a man's *best* was only *just good enough.* Every day he personally inspected the work in the foundry. Only metal castings that were accurate to 1/1000th of an inch suited him. Then he tested them further by flinging them to the floor. If they didn't break, he was satisfied. But too often the floor was cluttered with broken castings.

When it came to quality Henry Leland would not — indeed could not — settle for less than perfection. "Try again. You can do better," he assured his boys. Then he ordered the broken pieces returned for remelting.

When this had gone on for several months, the skilled machinists and their supervisors became thoroughly exasperated. One such worker was Horace Dodge who with his brother John would eventually open his own machine shop in Detroit and manufacture the Dodge car.

Feeling that Uncle Henry's stubborn demand for such superior quality was not only unreasonable but actually impossible, his boys made a desperate appeal to Mr. Faulconer. "He must be going crazy!" they complained bitterly. "His standards are too high for any foundry to meet!"

Deeply concerned, Mr. Faulconer pleaded with Henry to be less critical.

But when it came to quality, Henry Leland would compromise for no one. His prompt reply was positive and would, in fact, be widely quoted for decades. "There always was and there always will be a conflict between 'good' and 'good enough,' and in opening up a new business or a new department one can count upon meeting this resistance to high standards of workmanship," he said. "It is easy to get cooperation for mediocre work, but one must sweat blood for a chance to produce a superior product." After that the castings at "L & F" were perfect.

News of Leland's supreme quality spread throughout Detroit. It even reached the small town of Dearborn where Henry Ford was building his first car.

Fittingly enough, manufacturers began paying up to three times more for a prompt delivery of "L & F" castings because they were accurate to 1/1000th of an inch and would not break if accidentally dropped. Soon competitors were forced to improve the quality of their products.

Leland developed a new way to grind casehardened bicycle gears so they were greatly improved and interchangeable. In addition, he began producing steam engines for streetcars, gasoline engines for boats, and adapting these internal combustion engines to many uses such as a motor for the clock at Detroit's City Hall.

In 1896 he rejoiced with fellow Republicans as William McKinley became President of the United States. That same year Ransom Olds of Lansing, Michigan, built his first gasoline-operated car. Three years later he moved to Detroit, built the first automobile factory on Jefferson Avenue near Belle Isle Bridge, and became the first manufacturer of mass-produced cars.

After months of struggling with the noisy transmission of his Curved Dash Oldsmobile, Mr. Olds asked Henry Leland for help. To Mr. Olds' great surprise, Leland made the transmission both quiet and interchangeable.

Consequently, when fire destroyed the Oldsmobile factory, Mr. Olds asked Leland to build 2,000 small, single-cylinder gasoline engines, and

Leland & Faulconer became the first company to produce a continuous supply of automobile parts machined to 1/1000th of an inch. This Olds-Leland agreement established a precedent that became a permanent practice of the automobile industry.

So the days passed and Leland continued to be a friend to good causes, contributing as generously as possible to various charities. Additionally, he conducted a campaign to raise $100,000 for the Salvation Army. He rejoiced anew when McKinley was re-elected President. But of all the triumphs Henry Leland experienced during that eventful decade, 1890-1900, none gave him greater joy than establishing an interdenominational Thanksgiving Service for Catholics, Jews and Protestants. The ceremony became an annual tradition in the Auto-mobile Capital of the World.

Chapter 9
The Cadillac Car

The first National Automobile Show had been held in New York City in 1900. Now, in 1901, Detroit was holding its first auto show. On the second day Henry and Wilfred Leland hurried down to the old Armory Building on Larned Street to look things over.

Henry's keen eyes missed nothing, and Wilfred's photographic mind permanently noted everything. Of special interest to them both was the Olds exhibit displaying two seemingly identical motors on a platform. Two large dials showed that both engines were running at equal speed.

Suddenly, as the Lelands stood watching, a slim man with deep-set eyes stepped forward. "Go up on the platform and look behind the motors," the stranger suggested, grinning.

They did. It amused them, too, to see that a

brake load had been applied to the flywheel of one of the motors to hold its speed down to that of the slower engine. Father and son exchanged smiles of proud assurance. The faster engine had been built by Leland & Faulconer. The slower one had been produced by Dodge Brothers.

Unknown to Henry and Wilfred Leland, the stranger at the auto show was 38-year-old Henry Ford. In after years their paths would cross again and again. But not until some years later when Henry Ford came to Henry Leland for advice about grinding pistons did they learn who he was.

In the days to come Leland & Faulconer became well-known not only throughout the United States but in several European countries as well. The automobile industry was thriving, too. Along with many other Americans, the Lelands bought their first car. The Curved Dash Oldsmobile was personally delivered to their home by its inventor, Ransom Olds.

Although the Lelands liked their new car, Henry often found it to be temperamental. He believed its 3 horsepower engine could be greatly improved by making a few important yet simple changes.

Grateful to Ransom Olds for the important contract and wanting to help him in return, Leland decided to delve into improving the engine. With his team of skilled engineers — Alanson Brush, Ernest E. Sweet, Fred Hawes, Frank Johnson, Walter Schwartz, Lyle Snell, Walter H. Phipps, and Clair

Owen — Leland spent the next few months enlarging the intake and exhaust valves, increasing the valve diameter, and regrinding the cam.

The result was startling. Leland & Faulconer had a new, reliable engine which delivered 10.25 horsepower — at that time the most powerful engine of its kind in existence. Remarkably, it had been built for less money than it cost to produce the 3 horsepower motor for Ransom Olds.

Excited, Henry and Wilfred wasted no time driving to Jefferson Avenue to present their unusual gift to the Olds Motor Works. However, the company's business manager Fred L. Smith, refused to accept the first-rate engine because of the cost of retooling.

Stunned and hurt, the Lelands departed with their engine. They had expected it to be accepted with open arms. Instead, it had been rejected. What were they to do with it now? Henry put the powerful engine into his own Oldsmobile and returned to business. But he could not shake off the notion that the engine would be useful to people.

Meanwhile, William Murphy and Lemuel Bowen of the Detroit Automobile Company — recently renamed the Henry Ford Company — were having difficulty getting a new car built. When their chief engineer Henry Ford resigned, they decided to go out of business. Because of Henry Leland's reputation for honesty and fair dealing, Mr. Murphy and Mr. Bowen asked him to appraise their equipment.

54

Consultation at Leland & Faulconer. Left to right, Frank Johnson, Walter Phipps, Wilfred Leland (back to camera), Ernest Sweet, and Henry Leland.

Henry agreed. He went to the plant at the corner of Cass and Amsterdam Avenues and carefully inspected and priced the machinery. At the same time he quickly noted several poor methods and layouts. Later he had a serious talk with Wilfred. In the end he told his son, "Here is our chance to put the new motor to good use."

The next day Henry asked some of his boys to remove the 10.25 horsepower engine from his Oldsmobile and replace it with a standard 3 horsepower motor. Then he and Wilfred tied the high-powered engine onto the rear of their car and drove to the Henry Ford Company.

In the meeting room Henry placed both the financial papers and the motor upon the table. In a powerful yet kindly voice he told the board of directors, "I have done what you asked me to do. But gentlemen, I believe you are making a great mistake in going out of business."

Never timid about sharing his thoughts on industry, he told the men he had great faith in the future success of the automobile business and offered sound advice about the art of precision manufacturing.

A smile played about his lips as he said, "I have brought you a motor which we worked out at L & F. It has three times the power of the Olds motor. Its parts are interchangeable, and it is *not* temperamental."

The wealthy directors laughed and regarded this distinguished, white-haired machinist — with full mustache and beard — with keen appreciation.

Leland continued. "I can make these motors for you at less cost than I make the others for the Olds Works."

Henry Leland inspired his listeners. They were impressed by his motor and his ideas about manufacturing. They quizzed him eagerly. He patiently answered the questions. In the end they decided they would stay in the automobile business only if Henry joined them and reorganized the company. Because he was convinced that the motor could be of use to people, Leland agreed.

The next Wednesday, on August 27, 1902, the directors held a second meeting. Leland was given a small share of stock, made a director, and awarded contracts to produce the motors, transmissions, and steering gears of the new car.

Only one problem remained. What would they name it?

Someone suggested it be called Leland. But Henry replied at once, "Our city recently celebrated its 200th birthday. I think we should name the car in honor of the French discoverer of Detroit, Antoine Cadillac.

Minutes later, the directors voted unanimously to name the car Cadillac, and the Cadillac Automobile Company was established.

The first Cadillac car was built at L & F. From the start, Leland insisted on high quality. "Yes boys, that's good," he told his workmen, "but it isn't quite good enough. We must make every piston so exact and every cylinder so exact that every piston will fit perfectly into every cylinder. Then, if anything happens to either, it can be replaced by another and the car owner will not be obliged to buy both cylinder and piston if only one should be injured."

There were times he'd caution, "This wrist pin must be made accurate to the half-thousandths of an inch. Its bearings must be made with the same precision. Then there will be a perfect fit and practically no wear-out to it. Otherwise, the slightest 'play' means early wear and destruction."

Many felt that all this extra fuss was wasteful. But Leland insisted, "While this method and the refinements that it secures is expensive for us, it is the only correct method. The advantages will be best appreciated by the motorist who on being obliged to replace parts of his car has usually — or always — found it necessary to call upon an expert to fit them."

He said repeatedly, "Cadillacs must be made to run, not just to sell. They must be as perfect as we can make them."

The first Cadillac car was completed on October 20, 1902. Amazingly, it had accurately-made, fully interchangeable parts — something the experts believed impossible. By the end of the year, two more Cadillacs had been completed at L & F. When the third National Automobile Show opened in New York City the following January, it included two Cadillacs — the Runabout Model A and a larger Model B. Both carried the coat of arms of the founder of Detroit. Today, that same emblem appears on every Cadillac.

Chapter 10
A School For Mechanics

The first car Henry Leland invented was an instant success in America. By the middle of 1903 forty-eight Cadillac agencies had sprung up across the nation, and the demand had spread to Europe. In London young Fred Bennett, a salesman at the Anglo-American Motor Company, read an ad for Cadillac. Impressed, he somehow talked his boss into buying one.

Soon afterward, the Midland Automobile Club sponsored a hill-climbing contest. Fred Bennett decided to enter the topless, one-cylinder runabout.

In those days American-built cars were looked upon as inferior to British cars. Sunrising Hill was said to be one of the most difficult moors in all England. But the Cadillac averaged 8.09 mph and won "The Best Yet" award.

Toward the end of 1903 the Automobile Club

of Great Britain and Ireland sponsored a 1,000-mile reliability contest. Again Bennett entered the Leland-built car. And sure enough, at the end of eight daily runs the Cadillac received the highest number of marks in its class for reliability. News of the American car's high performance quickly spread throughout England. Before long Fred Bennett became the manager of his own Cadillac agency in London.

By 1904 a dozen new motorcar companies had sprung up in Detroit, and the city was booming with the automobile industry. As car sales increased, Henry and Wilfred Leland were forced to spend more and more time at the Cadillac Automobile Company. New buildings were built and additional equipment installed. When a severe fire broke out, production was delayed for 30 days.

Henry Leland never planned to go into the automobile business. He was perfectly happy running his thriving machine shop and foundry. But finally he was persuaded by Mr. Bowen and Mr. Murphy to consolidate the Cadillac Automobile Company with Leland & Faulconer. Consequently, on the day after Christmas of 1904 Henry became production manager and Wilfred was made business manager of the new firm called the Cadillac Motor Car Company.

In 1905 the Olds Motor Works moved back to Lansing, Michigan, and Cadillac became Detroit's first permanent producer of motorcars. On the first day of August the Cadillac Motor Car Company produced its 8,000th automobile.

Now Leland and his team of loyal engineers began experimenting with glass-enclosed cars. Henry retained their first model for his own personal car, naming it "Osceola" after the famous Seminole Indian Chief whom he admired.

One day in 1906 Leland read about a 32-year-old Swedish-American toolmaker named Carl Edward Johannsen who, after years of experimenting, had developed the "Jo-block" gauges. He claimed they would eliminate, at the source, many imperfect parts that shouldn't be used.

No other American took Johannsen's invention seriously. But fittingly enough, Leland purchased "Jo-block" gauges from Sweden and taught his machinists at the Cadillac Motor Car Company how to use them.

Thanks to Henry Leland's foresightedness, it wasn't long before "Jo-block" gauges became so popular in this country that Johannsen left Sweden and came to American to open a factory in Poughkeepsie, New York, which was later purchased by Henry Ford. Today, Johannsen gauges are used the world over.

As the automobile industry continued to grow so did the need for skilled mechanics. Leland saw this situation as an opportunity to help his community and his country. Unaided by professional educators, he organized the first school for automobile mechanics.

When the Cadillac School of Applied Mechanics opened in May of 1907, its students had to be at least 18-years-old, but the age was later lowered to 16. Young men were accepted from all over the United States. Such subjects as trigonometry, physics, mechanical drawing, and blueprinting were studied for 6,000 hours over a period of about two years.

What Henry Leland stressed most was good character and successful living. He repeatedly told his students, "The one essential ingredient of success is mastery of one's self as well as one's job."

To encourage them, he gave nine $10 to $50 prizes for top grades and a $15 prize for being prompt and maintaining perfect attendance for six months. In addition, he offered a $100 prize to any student who was neither tardy nor absent throughout the entire two-year course.

During the last week of school, students were taught how to drive a car. Indeed, in 1915 Leland built a Cadillac with two brakes — one on the passenger side so he could stop the car, if necessary, while a student was driving.

After graduation, many of the first-class mechanics took an additional 3,000-hour course and then worked for the Cadillac Motor Car Company permanently. Others were given Leland's blessing and went to work for such companies as Dodge Brothers, Ford Motor Company, Hudson Motors, and Studebaker Corporation.

Many schools for mechanics are in existence in America today, and people around the world are indebted to Vermonter Henry Leland who had the vision to meet this crucial educational need.

Chapter 11
Rewarding Test

June of 1907 was a happy time for the Lelands. Gertrude became the wife of Angus Woodbridge, and Wilfred married Blanche Dewey. Both young couples made their homes on North Grand Boulevard in Detroit.

Meanwhile in London, Fred Bennett was having an exciting and busy time. The Cadillac continued to fascinate him. He had become convinced that the Leland-built car was the most reliable automobile in the world and decided to go to America to have a heart-to-heart talk with its creator. At the Cadillac Motor Car Company in Detroit Bennett was warmly welcomed by Leland and given a tour of the well-organized factory. A long friendship began with his visit.

Bennett and Leland were both determined, farsighted gentlemen. Despite the difference in their backgrounds, both men loved people yet hated carelessness and indifference. Furthermore, they were both too honest to be silent when they believed a professional mistake was being made.

Glowing and deeply impressed by Leland's supreme integrity, Bennett returned to England. One day soon afterward he paid a visit to the officers of the Royal Automobile Club.

"Several manufacturers are claiming that they can easily supply new car parts for broken ones," Bennett began. "But in truth, some machining and filing is usually necessary. I believe there is only one manufacturer who can produce interchangeable car parts."

Great Britain's automobile experts sat back and laughed loudly. "A new part could *never* be matched to an existing part!" one authority stated bluntly.

Another threw up his hands in a gesture of helplessness. "Some wear is inevitable."

"Interchangeability is neither practical nor desirable," a third officer snorted.

Undaunted, Bennett persisted. "I ask you to conduct a test for accuracy."

At first, the officers of the Royal Automobile Club were indifferent toward Bennett's request. But in the end they were persuaded to sponsor a "Standardization Test." They drew up a list of strict rules, sent them to the world's automobile manufacturers, and agreed to supervise an impartial experiment.

Only one manufacturer accepted the challenge.

On the last day of February of 1908 the air was thick and white with large, fluffy snowflakes. Members of the Royal Automobile Club's Technical Committee hurried to Bennett's warehouse on Heddon Street West where they carefully selected three runabouts from the eight new Cadillacs which had just been shipped from America.

They drove the new cars 23 miles across London to the club's new race track at Brooklands. Despite deepening snow, the Cadillacs completed 10 laps at an average speed of 34 mph. Satisfied that the cars were in perfect running order, the experts parked them inside a brick garage and locked the doors.

The following Monday mechanics began taking the cars apart. Only wrenches, screwdrivers, hammers, and pliers were used. All other tools were forbidden.

Two days later, every nut and bolt and screw had been removed from all three Cadillacs. Frames were piled high in a shed. Such parts as pistons, rods, rings, oil pumps, and clutch bands were heaped on the garage floor.

Now the mechanics thoroughly mixed up the more than 2,000 parts. They made three separate piles — each including parts for one complete car. Then they removed 89 parts from the three piles and replaced them with identical Cadillac parts from Bennett's stock.

The next day, still under the critical eyes of the British experts, the mechanics rebuilt three cars from the three piles of parts. Fitting, scraping, and grinding were not permitted. None was necessary, for all parts fitted together perfectly.

A week later officers of the Royal Automobile Club stared at the three odd-looking cars which stood ready to make the 500-mile test drive around Brooklands. The cars had different-colored hoods, mudguards, and bodies. Even the wheels varied. They were still dubious and insisted, "It's impossible! Such precision is simply impossible!"

They were profoundly mistaken. The cars started easily, ran smoothly at full throttle, and completed 500 miles at an average speed of 34 mph.

While the speechless authorities shook their heads in amazement, Fred Bennett grinned with proud assurance. The experiment had proved that parts of all automobiles — if precisely manufactured — could indeed be interchangeable.

London newspapers printed the results of the "Standardization Test" and Leland became world-famous at once. Cables and letters addressed simply "Henry Leland U.S.A." arrived at his home in Detroit. Critics of American-made cars were silenced, and the door to dependable American mass production was open at last.

In February of 1909 interchangeable car parts won Henry Leland and Cadillac the Dewar Trophy, the highest prize given to an automotive engineer. In those days the Dewar Trophy was considered the Nobel Prize for automotive achievement in the world.

Henry Leland's grandson Wilfred Leland, Jr. perched inside the Dewar Trophy, the most prestigious prize in the automobile world. Leland and Cadillac won the Trophy in 1909 for interchangeable car parts.

When Leland received the huge silver cup in London, he was asked how it was possible to manufacture cars with interchangeable parts. His eyes sparkled as he replied with ready wit, "It's a simple process. First of all, you must know what you are going to do. Second, you must know how you want to do it. And, thirdly, you must do it that way."

Henry M. Leland was America's first winner of the esteemed Dewar Trophy, and he felt deeply honored. His joy took tangible form in a privately published booklet of tribute to his workmen in which he did his best to share the glory of the prize with those who helped produce the Cadillac.

He arranged a surprise celebration. Placing the beautiful, engraved trophy in the lobby of the Cadillac factory, he shook hands with and humbly congratulated his boys — all 1,000 employees. To each of them he handed a printed copy of "To the Men in the Shop," saying "The honor belongs equally to every honest, sincere and conscientious member of this organization, no matter what his position, who has striven constantly and patiently to acquire and maintain in the work he is doing each day that fine accuracy which has made possible the absolute interchangeability of parts in Cadillac cars."

Chapter 12
Birth of an Electrical System

By the time Henry Leland was 66-years-old, he had become a powerful man, loved and trusted the world over. He was invited everywhere and visited factories in Germany, France and England.

Amid his thousand chores he organized the National Foundries Association and the American Institute of Weights and Measures. He was elected president of the Society of Automotive Engineers and re-elected for five consecutive years. In addition, he gave his best efforts to the National Association of Manufacturers and the American Society of Mechanical Engineers. And, as founder and president of the Detroit Citizens League he continued to fight against corruption in city government.

Although he felt gratified to have created a top quality car, above all things he was proud of being a good mechanic. In the automobile business seemingly insurmountable problems came thick and fast, and more and more he had to depend upon his son. Therefore, in the summer of 1909 he agreed to sell the Cadillac Motor Car Company to William C. Durant for $4,500,000 — the largest cash property sale ever to take place in the United States automobile industry at that time.

Will Durant had recently organized the General Motors Company and would later become known as the "godfather of the automobile business." He appreciated the tremendous bargain he had received. Still, he needed the famous father and son team in order to maintain Cadillac's high standards. So he arranged a meeting with them. "I want you to continue to run Cadillac exactly as though it were still your own," he suggested. "You will receive no directions from anyone."

Henry and Wilfred Leland considered the offer. For the first time in their lives, they were wealthy and could afford to retire. Certainly they deserved to rest. But because they were creators not investors, they agreed to continue managing the Cadillac plant.

Within 33 days, profits from the sale of Cadillacs totaled $2 million, and Will Durant had back nearly half his cash purchase price.

Christmas Day of 1910 dawned crisp, cold, and sunny. Peace and good will filled the hearts of every member of the close-knit Leland family. Around the Christmas table heads were bowed in joyous thanks. Later Henry read the Christmas Story from the old family Bible, carols were sung, and gifts were opened. Everyone was happy for Wilfred and Blanche who had recently purchased a lovely, country home on Lake Angelus called "Wilchester." But to Henry and Nelle, the highlight of this wondrous celebration was playing with their two-year-old grandson, Wilfred, Jr.

Unknown to them, that same afternoon a lady was driving through Belle Isle Park. In those days, it was considered reckless for a woman to drive a car without a male passenger, for if the motor stalled, it could prove a dangerous task to start it again.

First, she must put the engine out of gear so that the car wouldn't run over her when the motor started. Then she must retard the spark and advance the throttle just the right amount. Next came the difficult hand cranking to turn over the motor. If the spark finally caught and the motor fired, she must immediately run from the front of the car to the right-sided steering column to advance the spark and retard the throttle. This must be done quickly. Otherwise, the engine would stop, and the long process would have to be repeated. Worst of all was the danger of the motor backfiring, thus causing a backward kick of the hand crank.

Still, this particular lady was never timid about driving alone. Her Cadillac easily bumped over the rough road which wound through the park. But as she approached a steep hill leading to an old wooden bridge over the Detroit River, she slowed down cautiously. And to her dismay the motor stalled.

A man named Bryon Carter was also enjoying a pleasant drive through Belle Isle Park on this Christmas Day. When he saw a lady standing beside her car, he immediately guessed what was wrong. He jammed on his brakes and offered to help.

He began to crank the car for her. Unfortunately, he assumed that she'd already retarded the spark. She had not. Suddenly the motor backfired and the hand crank kicked backward, striking him hard in the face and arm.

Soon afterward Mr. and Mrs. Ernest Sweet and Mr. and Mrs. Bill Foltz came driving by. Seeing Mr. Carter's bleeding face, the men sprang from their car, started the motor for the lady, then rushed the trembling man to the hospital. His face was badly cut, and his arm and jaw were broken. But the Cadillac engineers were assured that Mr. Carter would soon be all right.

Deeply concerned, Ernest Sweet wasted no time telling Leland what had happened. Henry's eyes blazed, and he burst out furiously, "Those visious cranks! I'm sorry I ever built an automobile. I won't have Cadillacs hurting people that way."

A few days later, Mr. Carter took a turn for the worse. Soon afterward he died of pneumonia. His death was a severe shock to Leland. For days, he seemed unable to think clearly. When at last his depression lifted and he was able to concentrate again, ideas for a mechanical starter began to race through his head.

He arranged a conference with his engineers. "The Cadillac car will kill no more men if we can help it," he told them in a husky voice. Then he gave them a tough assignment. "Lay all the other projects aside. We're going to develop a foolproof device for starting Cadillac motors."

A foremost research team working meticulously, the loyal engineers got busy at once. First, they studied the many early attempts to develop a self-starter, none of which had proved practical or dependable. Then they investigated new ways to build one. They soon became convinced that an electrical device with a starter motor and generator combined in one unit offered the most hope. In the end they discovered that suitable batteries were capable of operating the starting device, and the generator would keep the batteries properly charged.

Through the days of trial and error Leland guided his engineers with patience and integrity. Then came the summer day they asked an important question. Would the new Cadillac with its self-starter have a hand crank? Most agreed that it should.

Leland was delighted by the question. "Why not take it off? Haven't you any faith in your starter?" He smiled reassuringly despite their doubtful expressions. His eyes were teasing as he confided to them, "I removed the hand crank from the test car two months ago and hid it. No one missed it."

Another problem was that the experimental

motor was too big. It simply would not fit under the hood of the test car. How could they build a smaller one?

Assistant Sales Manager Earl C. Howard had a suggestion. "When I worked at the National Cash Register Company," he told Wilfred, "a man named Charles Kettering invented a very small electric motor for operating cash registers. Perhaps his experience would be helpful."

Wilfred went straight to the telephone and placed a call to Dayton, Ohio. The next day 34-year-old Kettering arrived at the Cadillac plant to study the electrical starting device built by Leland and his engineers. Impressed, Kettering agreed to try to improve his earlier invention.

Back in Ohio, the ambitious electrical genius gave up his job at the National Cash Register Company to work on the ignition system. In a short time he built a small motor with high turning power and an over-running clutch.

On Monday, February 27, 1911, Kettering returned to Detroit with the new motor. At the Cadillac plant the team of eminent engineers leaned forward as the motor was placed under the hood of the test car. It fit perfectly. But would it work? They waited breathlessly until the switch was pressed.

It worked!

Deeply satisfied, Henry and Wilfred Leland shook hands with and congratulated Charles Kettering. "I am very glad to have had the opportunity to be of some help in this important development,"

1912 Cadillac five-passenger touring car

Kettering replied humbly, "but the Cadillac engineers deserve the chief credit."

Then the Lelands praised the precision workmanship of Director of Engineering Ernest Sweet and Chief Engineer Fred Hawes as well as that of Frank Johnson, Lyle Snell, Herman Schwarze, D. T. Randall, Herman Zannoth, and R. T. Wingo. It was a happy day for them all.

A driving perfectionist, Henry Leland was now convinced that they could somehow improve Cadillac further. On windy nights one might use as many as two dozen matches trying to light the lamps of one's car. The ignition was powered by battery. Why not take the acetylene tank off the running board and give Cadillac electric lights? Was it possible to incorporate everything into one electrical system?

Leland discussed these ideas with his engineers. Consequently, Kettering went back to his laboratories in Ohio to try to advance these concepts. On several occasions Leland sent Ernest Sweet and Clair Owen to Dayton to assist him. In a remarkably short time they developed a reliable electric light system for Cadillac.

Because the Cadillac division of General Motors was running at full capacity and funds for expansion had not yet been approved, Leland contracted with the Dayton Engineering Laboratories Company in Ohio for 5,000 electrical starting, lighting, and ignition systems. But the exclusive right to the mechanism belonged to Cadillac.

1912 Cadillac roadster

In August 1911 Cadillac announced its self-starter. Almost at once rumors spread across the nation. Rival manufacturers called the self-starter a "half-baked invention" and "unreliable and troublesome." Worst of all, some insisted that self-starting cars attracted lightning and that drivers had been electrocuted.

For one so diligent and compassionate as Leland, this talk was infuriating. But Leland would not take any chances. He arranged for three electrical engineers from the General Electric Company to conduct an intense two-day test. They overwhelmingly approved Cadillac's electrical system.

In 1912 Cadillac was the only car with a dependable self-starter. The Royal Automobile Club made exhaustive tests of the new features. Again, they awarded the Dewar Trophy to Henry Leland and Cadillac, this time for his sponsorship of electric starting, lighting, and ignition — or the "Delco System" as it was named for the Dayton Engineering Laboratories Company. Henry Leland and Cadillac were the only man and car to win the international prize twice.

Because Leland wished to share all good things, he agreed to let other automobile manufacturers use the electrical layout. Before long many automobile companies adopted the "Delco System." Today this standard mechanism is an integral part of the automobile industry.

Chapter 13
The Secret Engine

Wilfred Leland's unwavering loyalty to his father was well-known. On several occasions his lightning-quick mind and diplomatic manner had saved the Cadillac Motor Car Company — and later General Motors — from bankruptcy. Because of his son's ceaseless help, Henry Leland was able to continue working long after most men his age had retired.

In 1913, as always, his father's foremost problem commanded Wilfred's attention. All over America people wanted bigger and heavier closed cars with more powerful engines. Six-cylinder motors with long, troublesome crankshafts far from satisfied Henry Leland. He speculated that a more efficient and refined engine might be possible if a way could be found to shorten the crankshaft.

Suddenly, in the middle of the night, an idea

struck Wilfred like a thunderbolt. Why not join two four-cylinder engines at a 90-degree angle?

The next morning Wilfred felt sure he had stumbled on an important discovery. Driving to work at top speed, he grew more and more excited. Once at the Cadillac plant, he headed straight for his father's office.

"We had good success with our four-cylinder motors," he began briskly, "so we would surely have equally good results with blocks of lighter four-cylinders and pistons by putting two of the blocks together at an angle and avoiding a long crankshaft."

If Henry Leland had wondered in the past whether he had been right to interrupt his son's promising medical career, he now felt positive that it had been meant to be. He looked at his 44-year-old son with pride. "I believe you've found the answer!" he declared triumphantly.

Right away he arranged an engineering conference so Wilfred could explain his concept of the V-8 motor. Ernest Sweet and the others shared Henry's enthusiasm and agreed to begin experiments at once.

The proposed motor was so special to the Lelands that they were determined to keep it a secret. They rented offices on the 22nd floor of the new Dime Bank Building opposite Detroit City Hall and transferred the experimental work there.

To help conceal their secret, they hired a British engineer named D. McCall White. The young Royal

Technical College graduate was placed in charge of design, and several additional engineers were employed.

"Leave no stone unturned," Leland instructed them. "Make every possible investigation, and maintain Cadillac's customary exacting standard."

The secret group worked at top speed. In an amazingly short time they designed fewer but larger crankshaft bearings, a new lubrication system, and a multiple-disc clutch. Furthermore, they placed the transmission on the engine, making the two items a single part to assemble.

At last the designing of the secret project was finished, and they started to assemble the experimental V-8 motor. The result was startling. Shorter and 50 pounds lighter than the four-cylinder motor, at high speeds it quietly delivered power without vibrating while maintaining good torsion at low speeds.

Then sorrow struck. After 46 years of marriage, Henry Leland's beloved Nelle died of cancer. No husband could have cherished his wife more, and his devotion to her never wavered. He grieved silently and grew more deeply devout. In the days to come it was a great comfort that his daughter Gertrude lived next door because she looked after him lovingly. He ate his meals there and took pride and joy in watching his two lively granddaughters, Miriam and little Gertrude, grow. On several occasions his son-in-law Angus accompanied him to various churches, schools, and engineering meetings when he spoke publicly.

Now human suffering became Leland's dominant concern. For the rest of his life, he gave more than half his annual salary to various charities, hospitals, homes, missions, and Christian schools.

In September of 1914 Cadillac announced quality production of the highly developed V-8 motor. This announcement began attracting attention from automobile journals and engineering societies. "The more cylinders the more trouble," it was noted. "The V-8 will never win over four and six-cylinders. Mechanics won't know how to repair them."

Competitors and conservative engineers continued to criticize Cadillac's new motor until Leland's essay, "The Penalty of Leadership" appeared in the *Saturday Evening Post*. It began, "In every field of endeavor, he who is first must perpetually live in the white light of publicity. Whether the leadership be vested in a man or in a manufactured product, emulation and envy are ever at work."

He concluded the message to his fellow Americans by saying, "That which is good or great makes itself known, no matter how loud the clamor of denial. That which deserves to live — lives."

Those were truly prophetic words. Cadillac's V-8 motor gave America a superior measure of engine performance. Proclaimed an extraordinary achievement, a Cadillac V-8 engine was placed in the Smithsonian Institute at Washington, D.C. As

The Cadillac V-8 engine, the brainchild of Wilfred Leland.

early as 1918, some 22 different automobile companies had adopted the V-8. Gradually, all automotive engineers came to accept Leland's sensible opinion on the importance of a short crankshaft.

That Henry Leland's only son had earned the respect and admiration of Cadillac's engineering staff was evident at a dinner given in his honor. He received a platinum plaque embossed with a gold replica of the first Cadillac V-8 engine. The inscription read: "To Wilfred Leland in recognition of his conception of the high speed, high efficiency V-8 engine and its application to the motorcar."

After a trip abroad in 1913, Henry confided to relatives and friends, "Soon Germany and Great Britain will be locked in the bloodiest war in history, and unless we intervene our present civilization may be destroyed." The people of the United States didn't agree with him, but it was an amazingly apt prophecy.

After war broke out in 1914, Leland went to the White House to speak with the nation's leader. "Mr. President, the war in Europe is America's war, too," he said with concern.

President Woodrow Wilson frowned. "It is none of America's affair," he contradicted.

"But, Mr. President, this country *must* prepare for the inevitable struggle," Leland warned. "We have to provide means for mastery of the air."

Believing that America should remain neutral, and busy with his campaign for re-election, President Wilson became somewhat annoyed. "Don't

Henry's son Wilfred C. Leland at age 80. On the wall at his left is the platinum plaque awarded him for his conception of the V-8 motor in 1914. The award was made in 1916. The bronze bust is Abraham Lincoln by Bissels, one of two in existence, and part of Henry Leland's extensive Lincolniana collection.

worry, Leland, I'll keep America out of war," he said briskly.

Although Leland hated war, he thought that in this matter the President was mistaken. "How," he asked his son later, "does Wilson think he can avoid war? America must join the fight sooner or later. We should be producing airplanes this very moment."

While the war rumbled closer, important matters at the Cadillac division of General Motors continued to claim Leland's attention. He rarely left his office before 10 o'clock each evening. One such problem was the electric lights on automobiles. They now shone so brightly that they blinded oncoming motorists. Ordinances had recently been passed which required drivers to stop outside cities and towns to cover their headlights with handkerchiefs or paper. Cadillac engineers worked diligently trying to find a solution to the annoying problem. By 1915 they had invented tilt-beam headlights.

Chapter 14

Homecoming

In the days to come, Leland found that more and more his thoughts wandered back to Vermont. How he longed to return to Barton. But it seemed there was never enough time to do everything he needed to do.

Over the years, he had corresponded with his cousin Leona Leland Leonard, who lived on a dairy farm in Barton. In spite of the Lelands' almost overwhelming responsibilities during the summer of 1916, Henry and Wilfred decided to pay Leona and her family a visit.

It was good to be back in Vermont again. The Leonards and Lelands spent a happy day together, then Wilfred drove his Cadillac up the steep, narrow road to the Timothy Dudley farm which had been his father's boyhood home.

With a happy heart, Henry led Wilfred past the old farmhouse to the apple orchard, and to the pasture beyond where Morgan horses grazed.

Henry's love for horses never ended. A picture was taken of him sitting on his riding horse which appeared on the front page of a magazine called the *Lincolnian*. And Wilfred owned thoroughbreds named Nina and Rigel.

Henry hiked over the hill and gazed fondly at the town of Barton far below. Then they visited the hilltop cemetery and searched for names of relatives and friends on gravestones. Finally, they strolled along Roaring Brook and visited the old schoolhouse which Henry had attended at the age of six.

With Leona's help, Henry arranged a family reunion at the Hotel Orleans. Nearly every member of the Leland family who lived in northeastern Vermont attended. Henry was heartened by the warmth with which his unknown cousins and their families welcomed him. He, in turn, delighted everyone with his extraordinary height and exciting stories.

Too soon it was time to return to Detroit. But Henry Leland would cherish the memory of those summer days in Vermont for the rest of his life. He planned to return when the autumn foliage was most impressive but never did. And he deeply regretted not being able to get away to attend the 125th anniversary of the settlement of Barton to which he was invited as an honored guest in 1921.

Top: Henry Leland and son Wilfred examining partridge feathers in hillside meadow in Barton, Vermont. Bottom: Wilfred Leland and his wife Blanche and Henry Leland and his daughter Gertrude Leland Woodbridge at Roaring Brook, Barton, Vermont.

However, he did not forget his relatives. He wrote to his cousins and sent them books, magazines, stereopticon views, and Christmas greetings.

Chapter 15
A Loyal American

Thanks to members of the Detroit Citizens League, the Automobile Capital of the World held its first honest election in many years on November 7, 1916. It was a great satisfaction to the League's founder Henry Leland that in less than six years city government had been reorganized and corrupt politicians ousted. In all he would serve as the League's president for 14 consecutive years until he was 82-years-old.

Meanwhile, the international situation worsened. Early in 1917 German submarines began attacking United States ships. Americans were outraged and demanded war. Finally, President Wilson acknowledged the threat to this country. On April 6, 1917, the United States declared war on Germany.

Henry Leland was convinced that the Cadillac

division of General Motors should begin producing airplane engines at once. His son agreed. So the day after war was declared Wilfred traveled to New York to have a talk with Will Durant.

"Cadillac has just completed a large building on Clarke Avenue," Wilfred began. "We had planned to build bodies for closed cars there, but couldn't we use the space to build fighter airplane engines instead?"

An expression of indignation crossed Mr. Durant's face. "This is nonsense!" he snapped. "This war should stop tomorrow."

"But we must help win this war," Wilfred reminded him, "or our children will have to fight it out later. This is our war now."

With an icy voice, Mr. Durant retorted, "I don't care for your platitudes. This is *not* our war, and I won't permit any General Motors unit to do work for the government."

When Wilfred returned to Detroit and told his father what Will Durant said, the lid blew off the old gentleman's emotions. "What!" he thundered, leaping forward. "He refused? How dare he deny his duty as an American citizen? Where is his patriotism?"

He scowled deeply in frustration, and tugged at his white beard. "We'll build our own factory," he blurted out. "If God has put me in a position in any way to shorten the war — if only by a few minutes — then I shall not have lived in vain but have fulfilled a great purpose."

Without hesitating even for a moment to consider the enormous personal cost, the Lelands began making independent plans. On Monday, June 18, 1917, they sadly resigned from the organization they had created. At the farewell dinner given in his honor Henry Leland soberly told his boys: "The Cadillac has been dearer to me than any other thing in the world except my home, but there has arisen now a claim on my loyalty that is nearer and dearer still. I do not believe the people of this country realize the monumental nature of their task. The time is coming, though, when this realization will be forced upon us." With deep emotion, he added, "The world's greatest need at this point is America; and America's paramount need now is to provide means for mastery of the air."

The Lelands left immediately for Washington to offer their talents to the government. "If you will assign us to it," Henry told General George Squier of the Air Service, "we will be glad to build a plant and produce as many airplane motors, of at least as good quality, as any manufacturer already organized to do so. We don't have a factory yet," he admitted, "but we have the means and knowledge."

The supervisor of aviation was greatly impressed by Leland's generous offer, but the War Department was almost totally unprepared. Neither a powerful aircraft engine nor a standard government contract had been prepared. The Lelands felt strongly that precious time was being wasted on formality and red tape. They went back to Detroit and

Superb father-son working team. Wilfred Leland, standing, with his father Henry Leland, seated.

spent their entire fortune purchasing and remodeling several small factory buildings on Holden Avenue.

A few days later, Will Durant came to Detroit. He had realized his mistake and decided to permit limited aircraft production at General Motors. He pleaded with the Lelands to return as managers of the Cadillac division. But it was too late. They had spent more than $300,000. Besides, they didn't believe in limitations when Americans were in danger of losing their freedom.

There were others who felt as the Lelands did. Among them were trusted friends and former employees such as Charlie Martens, John Boyer, William Murphy, John Trix, Ernest Sweet, John Emmert, George Laying, William Guy, Frank Johnson, George Nash and Charles Kettering. When they asked to join the new business, the Lelands gratefully accepted their help.

When it was time to select a name for the new organization, the Leland Motor Company was a popular choice. But Henry quickly said, "When I was a mechanic back in the days of my youth, I worked my heart out making guns for President Lincoln. If this organization honors anyone, it should be Lincoln. He was the finest man who ever lived in America!"

The firm was named the Lincoln Motor Company.

Another loyal American was Jesse G. Vincent of the Packard Motor Company. For many years he had experimented with a powerful race car motor similar to an airplane engine. Now he offered it to the United States Government. It was gratefully accepted, and christened the "Liberty" motor.

In three months, the small Lincoln factory on Holden Avenue was equipped to produce 14 Liberty motors a day. But Washington was still in a state of confusion. Soon aviation officials were begging the Lelands to produce 100 engines a day. The Lelands were stumped. There was no way they could increase production that much unless they built a huge, new factory. But they had spent their entire fortune and had no money left. The government could have made arrangements with existing automobile firms. Instead, its representatives urged the Lelands to accept a government loan to build a new factory.

Believing that no sacrifice was too great when civilization was at stake, the Lelands were easily persuaded. Hurried meetings were held, and 55 acres of land on Warren Avenue were purchased. In the amazingly short time of four months they built an enormous, brick factory consisting of eight buildings. Its main structure was four stories high and three city blocks long.

Finally, on the last day of August 1917 the Lincoln Motor Company signed the first United States Liberty motor contract for 6,000 engines. Four days later the Packard Motor Company signed a similar contract for the same number. Soon afterward the Ford Motor Company agreed to produce 5,000, and various other organizations signed contracts for smaller amounts.

At 74, Henry Leland drove himself as hard as any young soldier one-third his age who fought on the battlefields. High quality, more vital than ever, became harder and harder to maintain. The War Department made 1,398 changes in the Liberty engine's design, and production was constantly interrupted while expensive tools and machinery were altered or replaced. Skilled mechanics were almost impossible to find and keep during wartime. Unfortunately, the inexperienced help too often lacked patience and sense of purpose so necessary for precision work, and the turnover of employees was astonishing.

Furthermore, the government made several changes in United States Liberty motor contracts. In December of 1917, the Lelands signed a modified contract. Then, on the last day of July 1918, they signed still another which called for 9,000 engines at $4,000 each, plus an additional 8,000 at $4,000 if needed — 17,000 in all.

Under these extraordinary conditions, it was almost impossible to get into production. Nevertheless, within a year employment at the Lincoln Motor Company rose from 142 to 6,000, and 2,000 fighter aircraft engines were produced. In all the Lincoln Motor Company manufactured 6,500 Liberty motors — more than any other organization — at the lowest cost of $2,900 per engine.

Many years later Henry Leland looked back on

those hectic war days with a profound sense of pride. "Beautiful engines they were," he said with enthusiasm. "I felt I was doing a real service."

At last the most dreadful war in history ended with the signing of the Armistice on November 11, 1918. Across the nation bands played and Americans danced in the city streets.

Henry Leland thanked God for peace.

Chapter 16
The Lincoln Car

Now that World War I was over the United States Government asked the Lelands to cancel their non-cancellable Liberty motor contract. Even though it left them deeply in debt, they agreed. With the vanishing market for airplane engines, the huge Lincoln factory fell silent, and 6,000 men and women were jobless.

One evening early in 1919 Gertrude quizzed her aging father about his future plans. "Surely you'll retire now," she pleaded.

"I have no intentions of retiring," he promptly replied.

"But Father," she objected, "you're 76-years-old. You've worked so long and hard. You deserve to take it easy now."

But Leland's eyes danced. "I'm thinking about building a new motorcar," he confided.

Later, when he discussed his ideas for a new car with Wilfred and the other Lincoln directors, they immediately caught the glow of his enthusiasm. The company was reorganized and new stock placed on the market. Within three hours, $6,500,000 of Lincoln stock was sold.

Leland often said, "A man's best is only just good enough." In 1902 he'd believed that the Cadillac car was his very best effort. But now he was positive he could top even his best. The second automobile that Henry Leland created was an exclusive luxury car of meticulously crafted metal. Its simple lines were designed by his son-in-law Angus Woodbridge, and it had a durable chassis and a flawless V-8 motor with parts machined to 1/10th the diameter of a piece of fine human hair.

With a smile of proud assurance Henry Leland declared, "It's the finest motorcar ever built!"

His associates thought so, too, and insisted that the automobile be named after him. But Leland spoke firmly. "Abraham Lincoln was the finest man who ever walked this land. It should be named after him." Leland had his way and the automobile was called the Lincoln. But Henry was persuaded to stamp "Leland-built" on the V-8 engines of every first-year model.

Even before the Lincoln was exhibited 1,500 orders with deposits were placed for roadsters, limousines, and town and touring cars. Soon the huge factory bustled with activity as 6,000 workers who'd been without jobs for several months gratefully returned to work.

Then misfortune struck. First, several large shipments of quality materials were delayed because of a strike at Salem, Ohio. Then, the United States Treasury Department accused the Lincoln Motor Company of owing $5,725,673 in war profit taxes.

To men of the Lelands' outstanding integrity, the charge was especially humiliating. They had paid an honest $4,126,000 to the government in 1918. Nevertheless, they were forced to spend precious time in Washington while their accounting records were slowly and thoroughly investigated. In the end government officials stated that no more tax was due, and the claim was withdrawn. But the lengthy delay was to prove disastrous.

When the post-war recession hit the nation, Americans everywhere cancelled car orders and demanded their money back. Factories sharply decreased production, and employees' hours were cut back to part-time. Many factories — including the Ford Motor Company — were forced to shut down.

Prices were slashed. Still, instead of an expected 6,000 only 700 Lincolns were sold in the fall of 1920. The directors began to panic. But Henry Leland was positive that with patience and faith Americans could work out their financial difficulties. He was equally sure that the Lincoln motorcar was a winner.

To meet some pressing bills, though, he needed money badly. Unless financing could be arranged

1921 Leland Lincoln five-passenger sedan, Model 105. From the collections of Henry Ford Museum and Greenfield Village.

soon, the small stockholders, who were old friends, could be dreadfully hurt — some even impoverished. No one had ever lost money investing in him. He was determined to try to keep that record. Disheartened but undaunted, the Lelands made several unsuccessful attempts to secure financing. Finally, Wilfred found a banker who was willing to consider a $10 million loan. With hopes high, the Lelands rode the train to New York.

It proved to be an idle hope. Just as Wilfred entered his reserved room at the Belmont Hotel, the telephone rang. It was his secretary in Detroit. She said, "The company just received another tax bill for $4,500,000." With heavy hearts, the Lelands kept their appointment at the bank. But they were too honest to withhold information. When Wilfred broke the bad news before the loan was even discussed, the meeting was abruptly adjourned.

Some time later the government again announced that there was no evidence of dishonesty in the Lincoln income tax matter. But the announcement came too late.

About $30 million was invested in the Lincoln Motor Company. But all over America times were hard. Only such men as Henry Ford, Will Durant, Henry Goldman, and William Murphy had the means to even consider buying such a huge organization. And no one could possibly pay what it was worth.

When newspapers reported Leland's financial plight, the people of the United States prayed for him in churches across the nation.

Saturday, February 4, 1922, dawned cold and gloomy. By 9 o'clock in the morning hundreds of shivering people stood in the raw wind in front of the main Lincoln building. At exactly 11 o'clock a court officer began reading the long order of sale. The moment he finished the sun burst through the clouds, warming the hearts and faces of the 3,000 spectators. Then the bidding began.

An attorney quickly flung up his arms. "I bid eight million dollars for Henry Ford."

"We have a bid of eight million from Henry Ford," the auctioneer announced in a loud voice. "Are there any more bids?"

The huge crowd was silent.

Then the auctioneer's gavel struck the table, and a cheer went up from the crowd. "Ford's got it! Ford's got it!" they shouted. The stirring notes of "Hail to the King" echoed over Detroit as a thousand well-wishers poured into the Lincoln lobby to shake hands with Henry Leland. Soon afterward at a desk near a flag-draped portrait of Abraham Lincoln, Henry and Wilfred Leland and Henry and Edsel Ford signed a legal contract making the Fords the new owners of the Lincoln Motor Company.

Sadly, the Lelands retired from the automobile industry forever. But Henry had forecast with amazing accuracy that the Lincoln motorcar was a winner. Soon the Lincoln Division became one of the foremost units of the Ford Motor Company. President Calvin Coolidge preferred the Lincoln car.

Henry Leland on his riding horse. This photograph, taken about 1910, appeared on the cover of the employee magazine *Lincolnian*.

And in the years to come, Lincoln limousines carried presidents, foreign heads of state, popes, royal families, and celebrities, thus establishing a tradition which persists to this day.

The car that Henry Leland named for the 16th President of the United States is still the favorite White House car and remains on roads all over America.

Chapter 17
"Detroit's Best Citizen"

On Friday, February 16, 1923, Henry Leland gingerly climbed the 433 steps to his office on the 22nd floor of the Dime Bank Building opposite Detroit City Hall. But he'd just begun to work at his desk when he was called back down to the ground floor. Surprised, he picked up his wooden cane and quickly descended the hundreds of steps he'd just climbed.

When he reached the lobby, it was full of people with gifts and flowers for his 80th birthday. Right away Henry's eloquent voice and soul-satisfying laugh filled the room. In a second everyone was talking and laughing, too, and shaking his huge hand. With a joyful heart, he thanked each old friend for remembering his special day.

When at last he turned and with springy step began climbing the 22 flights of stairs for the second time that day, he was followed by a swarm of newspaper reporters whose faces quickly began to grow red. Accordingly, when Leland flung open the door to his office, only a handful of weary reporters staggered in. Those few who had managed to keep pace with him stared at the aging gentleman in disbelief. "How," a middle-aged reporter gasped, "can anyone stay so young?"

Leland smiled. "One way," he replied earnestly, "is to begin work at the age of nine and keep a full head of steam for 70 years, using both hand and brain, and maintaining complete faith in God and man."

Almost to the end, Leland fought against corruption and what he called "the bad citizenship of good citizens." Two days after his 85th birthday, a magazine called *Manufacturer's Record* published his forceful article called " 'Personal Liberty' to Violate Law" against the lawlessness of the liquor traffic. And he continued to give sound mechanical assistance to inventors who asked his advice.

Loved and trusted, known around the world as "Detroit's Best Citizen" and the "Grand Old Man of Detroit," Leland received Honorary Doctorates from the University of Vermont and the University of Michigan. And not a day passed without his thoughts drifting to Vermont, and he often dropped a few lines to his cousins there.

Finally, a kidney ailment forced him to seek treatment at Detroit's Grace Hospital. During the next month, his incredible strength slowly faded.

On March 26, 1932, with his loving son by his side, Henry Martyn Leland died at the age of 89.

Today Cadillac is Detroit's oldest producer of automobiles, and Lincoln is the favorite White House car. But above all, Henry M. Leland was a patriotic American who helped millions of people "hunt for the right way and then go ahead," as he himself had been taught to do back in Vermont.

Henry Leland, at 73, sitting in open field in Barton, Vermont.

Works Consulted

Books

Bailey, Scott L. *General Motors: The First 75 Years of Transportation Products.* Detroit: General Motors Corporation, 1983.

Bentley, John. *Antique Automobiles.* Greenwich, Connecticut: Fawcett Books, 1952.

Clymer, Floyd. *Early American Automobiles.* New York: McGraw-Hill Book Company, Inc., 1950.

Cragg, Richard. *Birth of a Giant: The Men and Incidents That Gave American the Motorcar.* Philadelphia: Chilton Book Company, 1969.

Hendry, Maurice D. *Cadillac: The Complete Seventy Year History.* Automobile Quarterly Publication, 1973.

Henry, Maurice. *Lincoln: America's Car of State.* New York: Ballantine Books, Inc., 1971.

Leland, Mrs. Wilfred C. (Ottilie M.) *Master of Precision — Henry M. Leland.* Detroit: Wayne State University Press, 1966.

Leland, Sherman. *The Leland Magazine or a Genealogical Record of Henry Leland and His Descendants, 1653-1850.* Boston: Wier & White, 1850.

Articles

"Cadillac" Editorial. *Car Classics* (February 1977), 16-17.

"Cadillac 1914" Editorial. *Car Classics* (August 1967), 12-17.

George, Marion. "Henry Leland, Spirit of the Marque," *Car Classics* (February 1977), 25.

Hendry, Maurice D. "Cadillac From Model A to Seville, A History," *Car Classics* (February 1977), 20-24, 28-31.

"Henry Leland Dies in Detroit Hospital" Obituary. *Automobile Topics*, April 2, 1932, pp. 521 & 530.

"The History of Lincoln" Editorial. *Car Classics* (February 1972), 11-17, 75.

Huntington, Roger. "The Pioneer V-8," *Car Classics* (February 1977), 33.

"Leland-Built" Editorial. *Car Classics* (February 1972), 8-10, 70.

Leland, Henry M. " 'Personal Liberty' to Violate Law," *Manufacturers Record*, February 18, 1926, pp. 85-88.

Lovett, William P. "Old Vote Swappers' League Plots to Get Grip on City Again," *Detroit Saturday Night*, June 3, 1922, [n.p.].

Nimmo, H. M. "How Would You Like To Be Really Young at the Ripe Old Age of 79?" *Detroit Saturday Night*, July 8, 1922, pp. 2-3.

Pipp, E. G. "The Lincoln-Leland-Ford Deal," *Pipp's Weekly*, February 3, 1923, pp. 2-6, 14-15.

———. "The Vindication of the Lelands — What about the Fords?" *Pipp's Weekly*, February 3, 1923, pp. 8-9, 12.

Ross, David H. "1911 Cadillac: The End of an Era," *Car Classics* (April 1975), 52-55, 58.

Steinwedel, L. W. "Two Henrys and the Lincoln Legend," *Saturday Evening Post* (1975), 52-55.

"The White House Lincolns" Editorial. *Car Classics* (February 1972), 35-37.

Yates, Brock. "The Greatest American Cars," *American Heritage* (February-March 1986), 32-41.

Letters

Henry M. Leland, Detroit, Michigan, to Mrs. Leona Leland Leonard, Barton, Vermont. August 6, 1904; March 13, 1915; April 18, 1921; July 1, August 7, October 7, October 24, and November 5, 1930.

Wilfred C. Leland, Detroit, Michigan, to Mrs. Elmer Leonard, Barton, Vermont. December 18, 1916.

Mrs. Angus (Gertrude) C. Woodbridge (Henry Leland's daughter), Detroit, Michigan, to Miss Grace Leonard, Barton, Vermont. May 2, 1919; June 6, 1922.

Interviews

Grace and Roy Leonard. Barton, Vermont. 1962-1979.

Photographs

Cadillac Motor Car Division, General Motors Corporation. Vicki Longwish, Public Relations. P.O. Box 297, Detroit, Michigan, 48232.

The Edison Institute, Henry Ford Museum & Greenfield Village. Cynthia Reed-Miller, Assistant Curator-Graphics. P.O. Box 1970, Dearborn, Michigan, 48121.

Wilfred C. Leland. Stereopicon views, gift to Mrs. Leona Leland Leonard, Barton, Vermont, December 18, 1916.

National Rifle Association. Gary Putnam, Photography Department.

Gloria May Stoddard

About the Author

Gloria May Stoddard grew up on a farm in Irasburg, Vermont, one of eight children, and she won her first literary prize at the age of twelve. After working and studying at the University of Vermont, she began her writing career as a contributor to the *Newport Daily Express.*

She is the author of *Snowflake Bentley: Man of Science, Man of God,* and her writings have appeared in *Christian Herald, Women's Day, Good Reading, The Friend, Highlights for Children, Wee Wisdom,* and *Child Life.* She's also written "Norman Rockwell: The Illustrator Everyone Knows," which was published in a reading textbook.

Gloria is the mother of two and the grandmother of one, has studied writing at Chautauqua Institute in New York, and lectures part-time. She's an avid reader and enjoys walking, playing the piano, collecting art, and discovering wildlife near her home in Holland, Vermont.